Boxing Mentality

Psychological Lessons for Personal Excellence

Andrew Hudson

© **Copyright 2025 - All rights reserved.**

The content contained within this book may not be reproduced, duplicated or transmitted without direct written permission from the author or the publisher.

Under no circumstances will any blame or legal responsibility be held against the publisher, or author, for any damages, reparation, or monetary loss due to the information contained within this book, either directly or indirectly.

Legal Notice:
This book is copyright protected. It is only for personal use. You cannot amend, distribute, sell, use, quote or paraphrase any part, or the content within this book, without the consent of the author or publisher.

Disclaimer Notice:
Please note the information contained within this document is for educational and entertainment purposes only. All effort has been executed to present accurate, up to date, reliable, complete information. No warranties of any kind are declared or implied. Readers acknowledge that the author is not engaged in the rendering of legal, financial, medical or professional advice. The content within this book has been derived from various sources. Please consult a licensed professional before attempting any techniques outlined in this book.

By reading this document, the reader agrees that under no circumstances is the author responsible for any losses, direct or indirect, that are incurred as a result of the use of the information contained within this document, including, but not limited to, errors, omissions, or inaccuracies.

Table of Contents

Introduction 5
1. The Foundation of Mental Toughness 14
   Discipline and Dedication 17
   Confidence and Humility 20
   Focus and Concentration 23
   Resilience 26
   Adaptability 29
   Aggression and Self-Control 31
   Courage 33
2. Your Toughest Opponent 40
   Imposter Syndrome in Boxing 44
   Typical Triggers for Self-Doubt in Boxing 46
   Root Causes of Poor Self-Esteem 50
   How to Resolve Low Self-Esteem 65
3. Pursuing Results 74
   Trust The Process 76
   Shaping Your Identity 78
   Small Changes, Significant Results 91
4. Enhancing Cognitive Control 102
   Understanding Cognitive Control in Boxing 104
   Regulating Your Emotions in Boxing 109
   Concentration Techniques 112

Cognitive Training Exercises 137
Practical Exercises 153

5. Increasing Your Value 156
Understanding Self-Value 160
Tips to Boost Self-Esteem 164
Getting the Balance Right 166
Showing Your Confidence 169

6. Mental Conditioning and Preparation 173
Importance of Mental Conditioning and Preparation 175
Self-Reflective Questions 190

7. Beyond the Ring 195
Translating Boxing Principles Into Personal Success 196
Achieving Personal Excellence 199
Success Stories 202
Boxing Mentality in Daily Life 207

Conclusion 209
References 215

Introduction

In the brightly lit arena, the tension was running extremely high while two fighters prepared to pound each other in the middle of the ring. In the blue corner stood Robert, a seasoned campaigner famous for his ceaseless aggression and willpower. In the opposite red corner was Nelson, a promising youngster with some of the fastest reflexes the game had not seen for quite a while. He was a great fighter with a craving for success.

As the bell rang and the fight began, it quickly became obvious that Nelson was going to put up a fight of his life. With remarkable agility, he threw his punches in a fast and furious manner, frequently catching Robert off guard while occasionally sending him reeling backward. Despite his early setback, Robert was able to put up some fantastic resistance. He definitely was no stranger to adversity, and as he weathered the storm of blows, a steely resolve gradually settled over him.

With every round that passed, Robert's mental robustness became increasingly apparent. Regardless of the salvo of blows raining down upon his face, he remained resolute, determined not to falter, calling upon a reserve of internal power that appeared to grow stronger with every moment that went by. While Nelson's attacks grew more frenzied and desperate, Robert stayed cool and collected, his attention relentless even in the face of overwhelming odds.

As the last round beckoned, it was evident that the fight was hanging in the balance. The two protagonists were battered and bruised, their bodies aching and pushed to the brink of exhaustion. However, while Nelson's mood appeared to falter under the weight of fatigue, Robert's determination was stronger than before.

In a last-ditch attempt to steal a win, Nelson threw a flurry of punches at Robert, each one more vicious than the previous one. Despite this late barrage of punches, Robert drew upon every ounce of mental toughness within him, standing firm against the onslaught, his defenses impenetrable, his determination unyielding.

And then, in a moment that appeared to stretch on for eternity, Robert found his chance. With a superfast counterblow, he landed a debilitating punch to Nelson's chin, sending him sprawling to the canvas in one massive heap covered by sweat and blood. As the referee counted him out, the crowd went into a deafening frenzy, and Robert raised his arms in celebration: a fitting testament to the potency of mental toughness in the face of adversity.

In the unforgiving terrain of boxing, an environment where victory is mostly decided by split-second decisions and unyielding willpower, there is a force much stronger than sheer physical strength: A force generally known as mental toughness. In this book, you will learn the skills that are necessary for you to tap into the psyche of champions as well as the timeless wisdom that goes beyond the confines of the ring.

Imagine two fighters, evenly balanced in power and technique, stepping into the ring, their hearts pacing with anticipation. As the bell rings and the first round starts, it becomes certainly clear that success will not be determined by mere physicality alone. It is in the crucible of combat that the true measure of a fighter is revealed—not in the muscles that flex, but in the mind that perseveres.

Every victorious warrior has a reserve of mental toughness, an unflinching desire that pushes them through difficulties and toward achievement. This is the epitome of mental toughness, which is closely associated with boxing, much like the announcer's voice and the ringing of the bell.

But what really is mental toughness, and why is it so deeply intertwined with the sport of boxing? To comprehend this, you need to first remove the layers of history and look into the rich bond between psychology and boxing.

From the initial days of pugilism to the current era of prizefighting, the function of psychology in boxing has been as significant as the cross and the jab. Throughout the pages of boxing history, champions have not merely improved their physical techniques, but also honed their mental acuity, using psychological strategies to outclass and outmaneuver their adversaries.

It is inside the crucible of training and competition that the real importance of mental robustness becomes evident. In the difficult regimen that a boxer employs as they prepare to fight, where every punch thrown is a testament to discipline and dedication, mental toughness serves as the cornerstone upon which champions are forged.

But the relevance of the boxing mentality extends far beyond the confines of the ring. In today's world, where challenges abound and adversity lurks around every corner, the ability to cultivate mental toughness is not just desirable—it is essential.

In a society where comfort often breeds complacency and adversity is shunned rather than embraced, those who possess the resilience and fortitude of a boxer stand head and shoulders above the rest. In a world where mediocrity is the norm, the path to excellence lies in the unwavering pursuit of mental toughness.

And the benefits of acquiring such resilience are myriad. From improved performance in the ring to heightened self-image and confidence in all facets of life, the rewards of mastering the boxing mentality are as profound as they are far-reaching. But make no mistake—achieving mental toughness is no easy feat. It requires dedication, discipline, and a willingness to confront one's fears and limitations head-on. It is a journey fraught with challenges and setbacks, but one that promises untold rewards for those bold enough to embark upon it.

I am a boxing coach and psychological expert who is on a mission to help you become the best version of yourself. I do this by teaching the principles of boxing and publishing various self-help resources online for you to benefit from.

I take so much pride in what I do because there was a time when I was a man who struggled in life. My low self-esteem caused me to fear being wrong, preventing me from having any kind of success in my life. I managed to build self-esteem from boxing sessions, and as I overcame my previous mental-related issues, I developed a love for boxing and had a desire to deeply understand human behaviors.

I decided to write this book because I like to teach what works for me; I know what it feels like to suffer in silence and be lost in life. My teachings are very simple to follow, and I hope to reach a wider audience through publishing. I am just a normal guy who managed to overcome the darkness in his mind.

Before becoming the man I am today, I went through a lot of struggles as a young person. I faced rejection many times from employers and women, struggled with boxing training for many months when getting started, was slow to learn skills, and overall felt as if I was destined for failure.

I invite you to join me on a journey into the heart of the boxing psyche—a journey that promises to unlock the secrets of champions and empower you to reach new heights of personal mastery. Through a blend of historical insight, practical wisdom, and actionable advice, this book offers a roadmap to cultivating the mental toughness needed to succeed not only in the ring but in life itself.

So, are you ready to unleash the warrior within and embrace the transformative power of the boxing mentality? If so, then prepare yourself for a journey unlike any other—a journey toward unparalleled mental toughness and personal excellence. In the first chapter, you will learn about how to effectively create mental toughness.

The Boxing Training Handbook

A summary of essential boxing teachings, combining physical training techniques, practical drills, and key psychological lessons, in clear and concise points.

Follow the link below to download the handbook for **free**
www.subscribepage.io/boxingtraining

The Confidence Workbook

A hands-on guide containing 7 simple strategies designed to help you build self-esteem and develop confidence today.

Follow this link to get your **free** online copy
subscribepage.io/buildconfidence

1. The Foundation of Mental Toughness

Getting started with the foundation of success: mental toughness. In this chapter, you will take a tour through the important aspects that constitute the foundation of mental resilience, gaining inspiration from the world of boxing. From determination and discipline to courage and adaptability, you look at the characteristics that distinguish exceptional fighters and prepare them to face obstacles both inside and outside the ring.

Throughout this chapter, you'll look at the complexities of mental toughness, including its numerous aspects and importance in the quest for excellence. You'll find real-life boxing examples to demonstrate how these characteristics show in the champions' actions and attitudes. The goal of this guide is to motivate you to grow your own mental fortitude and reach your full potential by exploring the intersections of discipline, confidence, focus, and other factors. It is time for you to now examine the anatomy of mental toughness and discover the keys to reaching excellence in boxing and beyond.

In the never-ending search for victory within the squared circle, there is a silent power that separates the victors from the contenders: mental toughness. But what precisely is mental toughness, and why is it so important to boxers' success? Mental toughness is fundamentally described as the ability to persevere in the face of adversity, to keep focus and resolve in the midst of chaos, and to recover from setbacks with renewed enthusiasm. The fighters' undying determination propels them forward even when their bodies scream for rest and their brains plead for release.

Mental toughness is not just an important characteristic for boxers; it is necessary for success in all areas of life. In the furnace of combat, where every punch is a test of resolve and every round is a struggle of attrition, the conquerors are distinguished by their mental toughness.

Consider boxing's legendary champions, such as Muhammad Ali, who danced through the flames of adversity with a smile on his lips and a fire in his heart, or Mike Tyson, whose savagery in the ring was equaled only by his unbreakable spirit. These men were not only physically exceptional sportsmen; they were mental warriors with a steely will that could withstand any storm.

But the value of mental toughness goes far beyond the ring. The ability to face problems head-on and push through adversity distinguishes the great from the merely good in the never-ending pursuit of perfection, whether in sports, business, or life itself.

For boxers, mental toughness is the foundation upon which all other abilities are built. It's the steel in their spine, the fire in their belly, and the unshakeable conviction that no challenge is insurmountable. Without it, even the most skilled athletes will fail to reach their full potential.

Discipline and Dedication

Boxing brilliance is built on two pillars: discipline and determination. They are the unflinching dedication to your craft, the never-ending pursuit of improvement, and the unlimited passion to push beyond the limits of comfort and convenience.

At its core, discipline is the capacity to stick to a tight routine of training, food, and lifestyle choices in the face of temptation or adversity. It is the willingness to forego short-term pleasures in order to achieve long-term success, to choose greatness over everything else.

Dedication, on the other hand, is the relentless commitment to your goals and aspirations. It is the zeal to pour yourself wholeheartedly into the pursuit of greatness, to persevere in the face of drawbacks and challenges, and to never shake in the belief that victory lies within reach.

For boxers, discipline and dedication are not just desirable traits—they are essential components of success. In the rigorous world of boxing training, where every minute of every day is meticulously planned and executed, discipline is what separates the champions from the also-rans. It is the willingness to show up to the gym day in and day out, to push oneself to the limit, and to never settle for anything less than one's best.

Dedication is the passion to devote your entire life to the pursuit of greatness, to hang on and keep moving in the face of failures and hurdles, and to never give up faith in your capacity to succeed. Discipline and determination are not simply desirable attributes for boxers; they are necessary for success.

In the grueling world of boxing training, where every minute of the day is painstakingly planned and executed, discipline is what distinguishes champions from losers. It is the willingness to go to the gym every day, push yourself to the maximum, and never settle for anything less than your finest.

Take Floyd Mayweather Jr. as an example; he is perhaps one of the best boxers of all time. Mayweather, who is renowned for his flawless work ethic and commitment to his trade, is the perfect example of self-control and determination in action. Mayweather followed a rigorous training schedule throughout his illustrious career, choosing to focus on perfection over the distractions of celebrity and wealth. The outcome? A perfect record, several world titles in several weight classes, and a legacy that will live on for many more years.

The legendary boxer Manny Pacquiao also serves as an example of how discipline and commitment can overcome hardship. Pacquiao's ascent to fame was driven by an uncompromising dedication to his profession and an undying work ethic, which helped him go from modest origins in the Philippines to worldwide superstardom. Pacquiao persevered in his commitment to his objectives in the face of many obstacles and disappointments, solidifying his status as one of the greatest athletes of all time.

Discipline and determination isn't built overnight, it takes countless repetitions of turning up when you don't want to, saying no to instant gratification and consistently taking action on the tasks that take you closer toward your goal, no matter how challenging or uncomfortable. To become disciplined and dedicated, keep your main goal in mind and begin to identify what actions take you towards your goal one step at a time, breaking down big goals into smaller objectives is a great starter for building mental toughness.

Confidence and Humility

Two sides of the same coin, humility and confidence are necessary attributes that every great boxer needs to have in equal proportion. While humility makes sure that success does not breed complacency and that you stay open to development and improvement, confidence gives you the self-assurance and belief in your talents that are necessary to thrive.

At its core, confidence is the steadfast faith in yourself and your skills. It is the deep-seated belief that no task is too difficult, no opponent is invincible, and no obstacle is insurmountable. A confident boxer gives off an air of assurance and resolve, going into every match believing that success is not just possible, but inevitable.

Humility, on the other hand, is the recognition that success is not solely the result of your efforts, but also of the contributions of others and the vagaries of fate. Humble boxers approach their craft with a sense of gratitude and appreciation, acknowledging their strengths and weaknesses alike and remaining open to feedback and constructive criticism.

To compete at your best, you must strike a balance between confidence and humility. While excessive humility can result in self-doubt and hesitation, excessive confidence can lead to arrogance and complacency. You can only realize your full potential and become a great boxer by finding the ideal balance between the two.

Take Muhammad Ali, who is arguably the best boxer of all time, as an example. Ali was the picture of confidence in the ring, well-known for his audacious predictions and brazen bravado. Beneath his arrogance and bluster, though, Ali maintained his humility, always ready to give credit to his coaches, colleagues, and supporters for helping him succeed. Ali's ability to strike a fine mix between humility and confidence helped him become a global celebrity and win many admirers.

Manny Pacquiao is another example; his ascent from poverty in the Philippines to international superstardom is the stuff of legends. Given his aggressive fighting style and willingness to take on opponents of any height or stature, Pacquiao clearly believes in his own talents. Even with all of his achievements and world titles, Pacquiao maintains an incredibly modest demeanor, frequently crediting his staff, his faith, and his supporters for his success. Due to his unique combination of humility and confidence, Pacquiao has won over admirers worldwide and solidified his status as one of the greatest athletes of all time.

In the end, it is the delicate balance between confidence and humility that separates the good from the great in the world of boxing. By cultivating both qualities in equal measure, you can unlock their full potential and achieve greatness in the ring and beyond. For developing these attributes, work hard and appreciate what you have, although that may sound generic right now, more will be uncovered throughout this guide to ensure you can cultivate the right mindset to achieve the balance of the two.

Focus and Concentration

Focus and concentration are the cornerstones of boxing success, important skills that enable fighters to reach their full potential in both training and competition. Focus and concentration, defined as the ability to direct one's attention and energy toward a certain activity or objective, are the motivators behind every punch thrown, defensive technique done, and strategic choice made in the heat of combat.

In training, focus and concentration are essential for developing the technical skills and physical conditioning required to excel in the ring. Whether shadowboxing, hitting the heavy bag, or sparring with a partner, you must keep a laser-like focus on every action, breath, and sensation in order to strive for excellence and refinement.

Similarly, in competition, attention and concentration distinguish champions from mediocre performers. In the frenzied turmoil of the ring, where split-second decisions can spell the difference between win and defeat, you must stay entirely focused on the task at hand, filtering off distractions.

However, in today's society, where technology and social media are ubiquitous, it is becoming increasingly difficult to retain attention and concentration. The continual deluge of notifications, emails, and social media updates has resulted in a society with short attention spans and the inability to focus for long periods of time.

This issue provides a unique difficulty for boxers, as maintaining focus and concentration is more vital than ever in today's distracted society. The temptation to check your phone or surf social media between sparring rounds or during a training session can be overwhelming, resulting in poor performance and missed opportunities for progress.

To address this issue, many boxers are turning to mindfulness and mental training approaches to improve their attention and concentration. You can train your minds to filter out distractions and maintain a high level of focus and concentration both in and out of the ring by adding techniques like meditation, visualization, and deep breathing exercises into your training regimens.

Finally, the ability to sustain focus and concentration in boxing distinguishes the exceptional from the just mediocre. You can achieve success both inside and outside of the ring by understanding the value of these attributes and aggressively cultivating them, regardless of the distractions that may threaten to derail you.

Resilience

In the field of boxing, champions are defined by their resilience, or the capacity to recover from adversity stronger than before. It is the indomitable spirit that refuses to give up in the face of defeat, the steadfast determination to endure in the face of adversity, and the tireless pursuit of excellence regardless of the odds.

Resilience, defined as the ability to recover rapidly from challenges, enables you to weather the storms of defeat, injury, and setback, emerging stronger and more determined than ever before. It is the reluctance to let failure define you, the readiness to learn from your mistakes, and the determination to keep moving forward regardless of the hurdles in your path.

Throughout boxing history, there have been innumerable examples of fighters that personify the spirit of resilience. From Rocky Marciano, who overcame a lack of natural talent and size to become one of the greatest heavyweight champions of all time, to Manny Pacquiao, who rose from poverty in the Philippines to become a global superstar, these fighters have faced adversity head-on and triumphed against all odds.

However, perhaps the most prominent illustration of boxing resilience comes from the fictitious character Rocky Balboa, played by Sylvester Stallone in the legendary film franchise. In one of the series' most memorable quotations, Rocky focuses on the significance of perseverance, saying, *"It ain't about how hard you hit. It's about how hard you can get hit and keep moving forward"*.

These phrases capture the heart of boxing grit and serve as a rallying call for all fighters. They remind you that success in the ring is about more than talent or technique; it is also about the willingness to persevere in the face of adversity. In the end, the boxer who refuses to give up, no matter how many times they are knocked down, wins.

To summarize, boxing champions rely on resilience. It enables fighters to overcome difficulties, defy the odds, and achieve greatness in the face of adversity. Boxers who exemplify the spirit of perseverance can transcend their constraints and write their own narrative of triumph and victory, motivating others to do the same.

You will fail, you will get frustrated and at times you will feel as if what you are trying to achieve is impossible, the ability to keep pushing past these negative feelings and outcomes is where you build mental toughness and prove to yourself that you are capable of achieving whatever you put your mind to.

Adaptability

In the dynamic world of boxing, adaptability reigns supreme as the ability to adjust and thrive in ever-changing circumstances. It embodies the capacity to seamlessly transition between different training techniques, opponents' styles, and strategic approaches, ensuring a boxer's readiness to confront any challenge that may arise within and beyond the ring.

Defined as the skill to respond effectively to new situations or environments, adaptability empowers you to remain versatile and resilient amidst the multifaceted demands of the sport. It encompasses the flexibility to assimilate new training methodologies, refine existing skills, and innovate tactical approaches, all while maintaining a steadfast focus on continual improvement.

Boxing requires adaptability due to the variety of training strategies used to acquire a broad skill set. From shadowboxing to sparring, heavy bag work to speed drills, each training method has a specific purpose in improving your physical characteristics, technical proficiency, and mental fortitude. The ability to effortlessly shift between these many approaches allows you to develop a well-rounded skill set that can be applied to any situation you may experience in the ring.

Moreover, flexibility is crucial for you to successfully negotiate the wide variety of opponent styles you may face over your career. Any opponent poses a different set of obstacles, requiring flexibility and agility in both strategy and execution. These opponents range from aggressive brawlers to elusive counterpunchers, and from southpaw stylists to orthodox sluggers. It is easier for you to take advantage of openings, seize opportunities, and win when you can swiftly analyze and adjust to the fighting style of your opponents.

Adaptation is a critical component of boxing success, allowing you to survive in the face of heterogeneity in training approaches and opponents' tactics. You can reach your full potential and grasp the sweet science of boxing by improving your capacity to adapt and grow in response to changing situations.

Aggression and Self-Control

Aggression and self-control are the twin cornerstones of boxing, both necessary for success and mastery. Aggression, defined as the bold quest for dominance and win, stimulates your desire to test the limits of your physical and mental ability. In contrast, self-control is the controlled restraint and calm that allows you to properly channel your aggression, ensuring that you stay focused, strategic, and in control of your actions both inside and beyond the ring.

Self-control is critical in boxing because it allows you to channel your aggression in positive and useful ways. While aggression is a normal and necessary part of competitive combat sports like boxing, excessive aggression can lead to recklessness, weariness, and vulnerability to counterattacks. Practicing self-control can temper your aggression with accuracy, patience, and strategic decision-making, increasing your effectiveness while reducing your vulnerability to costly mistakes.

Furthermore, self-control is essential for displaying sportsmanship, professionalism, and respect for opponents, coaches, and referees. Emotions can run high during competition, and the distinction between forceful aggression and unsportsmanlike conduct can become blurred. By demonstrating self-control you are better able to handle these difficult situations with elegance, honesty, and respect for the sport's laws and traditions.

Boxing is an effective way to release aggression in a controlled and constructive manner. You may channel your violent impulses into focused, disciplined action thanks to the severe physical demands of training and competition, helping you relieve tension, build confidence, and cultivate mental toughness. Furthermore, the strict structure and regimen of boxing training instill self-discipline, perseverance, and resilience that carry over into other aspects of your life.

Many people make the mistake of labelling boxing an aggressive sport, while boxers may channel their aggression to boost their performance, boxing has never been an excuse for aggressive people to lash out on people. Often, those who box just to exert violence are punished or made unwelcome to further sessions. So, don't let this put you off from heading down to your local gym for a session.

Courage

Courage, often seen as the foundation of greatness, is the unflinching will to face fear, uncertainty, and hardship with bravery and determination. It is the driving force that motivates you to push yourself beyond your comfort zones, confront your inner demons, and go on journeys of self-discovery and personal progress. In the context of boxing, courage is essential from the minute you enter the gym.

The decision to pursue boxing, to subject yourself to the physical and mental hardships of training, and to face the unknown obstacles that await needs enormous fortitude. It entails confronting the fear of failure, judgment, and pain and deciding to move forward despite these barriers.

However, it is precisely this act of courage—the willingness to take the first step into the unknown—that builds the groundwork for transformation and development. For it is only by confronting our anxieties and pushing above our imagined limitations that we can reach our full potential and become great.

So, if you may be hesitant to begin your own boxing journey, I beseech you: Be the first to step up. Gather the bravery inside you to take that first step of faith, rise to the occasion, and set off on a journey of empowerment and self-discovery.

Recognize that you are not alone in your path—that numerous others have walked this way before you, confronted their anxieties, and emerged stronger, more resilient, and more empowered as a consequence. Recall that bravery is the willingness to act in spite of fear, not the lack of it.

So, embrace the anxiety, the uncertainty, and the challenge that lies ahead of you. True change takes place in these moments of daring, and the seeds of greatness are sown. Be the first to take the initiative, and allow your introduction to boxing serve as the catalyst for a lifetime of growth, fulfillment, and achievement. Next up are some hard hitting truths to hopefully push you towards making the first step in your journey.

Hard Hitting Truths

- **You are capable of more than you realize**: Believe in your potential and trust that you have the ability to achieve greatness. James "Cinderella Man" Braddock is a great example of someone who came from nothing to achieve greatness. In the boxing world during the Great Depression, Braddock was the underdog. He battled to support his family and was viewed as a fighter who had been through too much. Braddock overcame heavyweight champion Max Baer in 1935 to become the world heavyweight champion, pulling off an incredible comeback against all odds. How come you can't overcome your challenges and realize your dreams if James Braddock could rise above such difficulties and become a champion?

- **Success requires dedication and perseverance**: Embrace the journey and be willing to put in the hard work and effort required to reach your goals. Nobody gets lucky in boxing, you don't see the countless hours of hard work and the sleepless nights that go into the final product, understand if you want something then you have to give it 110%.

- **Failure is a natural part of the process**: Understand that setbacks and obstacles are inevitable, but they are also opportunities for growth and learning. One well-known example of a person who went through several setbacks before finding success is Thomas Edison, the man who invented the lightbulb. Edison is credited with multiple failed attempts prior to creating the durable, useful electric lightbulb. It has been said that he attempted more than a thousand times without success before producing a functional prototype. "I have not failed," Edison famously remarked when questioned about his shortcomings. "I've discovered ten thousand ineffective methods."

- **Consistency breeds success**: Stay committed to your goals and make consistent progress every day, no matter how small. James Clear overcame his baseball injury with habits and is now a successful businessman because of his extreme dedication to his goals. His book 'Atomic Habits' is a must read I may add.

- **Surround yourself with positivity**: Surround yourself with people who support and uplift you, and cultivate a positive mindset that fuels your drive for success. Former wrestler and popular actor Dwayne

"The Rock" Johnson surrounded himself with a network of family and friends who encouraged him to pursue his film career.

- **Believe in yourself**: Have confidence in your abilities and trust that you have what it takes to overcome any challenge that comes your way. The renowned tennis player Serena Williams personifies steadfast self-belief. She persevered in her will to accomplish and her belief in her ability in spite of hardships and injuries.

Don't forget that the road you take to get there defines your success, not the destination itself. Accept the process, stay focused on your goals, and never lose sight of the motivation and tenacity that propels your desire for achievement. Remember, everybody's road to success is different, just because other people appear to have easily reached their goals doesn't mean that is the case, everybody faces their own unique challenges and makes sacrifices to get to where they are. Stay focused on your own journey and regularly compare yourself to older versions of yourself.

As you wrap up your lesson on the facts that fuel the desire for boxing success, it's critical to consider the value of developing a support network, understanding the relationship between effort and outcome, and acknowledging the importance of personal accountability and self-worth.

As you move on in your life, remember that it is acceptable to seek assistance and guidance from others. Whether it's finding a mentor, joining a boxing club, or simply surrounding yourself with positive people, developing a strong support network can provide important encouragement and aid along the road.

Second, the notion "you get out what you put in" applies to all aspects of boxing and life in general. Success in the ring is directly proportionate to the effort, dedication, and devotion you put into your training. This statement is equally true in your personal life because the amount of energy and passion dedicated to a particular assignment determines its successful completion.

Remember that every punch thrown, mile run, and hour spent doing your craft helps you grow and improve as a boxer. Accept the grind, maintain discipline, and believe that your hard effort will be rewarded in the long term. Furthermore, while it is normal to seek validation and approval from others, you must know that the only opinion that truly matters is your own. Accepting that no one cares as much about your achievement as you do can seem freeing. It enables you to pursue your own course and define success on your own terms.

As you continue to traverse the fundamentals of life, keep in mind that success is a never-ending goal. Accept the trials, cherish the wins, and remain true to yourself along the way. With the correct mentality, support network, and unshakable commitment to perfection, there is no limit to what you can do with your life, whether you are in the ring or out of it.

2. Your Toughest Opponent

In your quest for boxing expertise, you read about how much success in the ring involves more than just physical prowess: It also requires mental fortitude, tenacity, and the determination to confront your inner demons. Building on the framework set in the last chapter, which discussed the significance of mental toughness and self-belief, you now turn your focus to possibly the most daunting opponent you will ever face as a boxer: yourself.

In this chapter, you'll look at the psychological barriers that often stand in your way of reaching your full potential. Through personal experiences, professional insights, and practical techniques, you will face the insidious nature of self-doubt, anxiety, and impostor syndrome, as well as how these inner demons emerge in the boxing environment.

You'll look at the underlying causes of low self-esteem, including childhood events, societal influences, and established beliefs that shape your judgments of yourselves and your skills. Drawing on the insights of renowned entrepreneur Alex Hormozi, you will handle some difficult truths about masculinity, vulnerability, and the significance of pushing outside of your comfort zone.

But be rest assured that this chapter isn't just about addressing your inner demons; it's about conquering them. You will equip yourself with practical tools and tactics to combat fear, self-doubt, and impostor syndrome, reclaiming your strength as a fighter.

Prepare yourself for a voyage into the depths of your own psyche: One that will challenge, inspire, and eventually empower you to overcome your inner demons and emerge victorious in the ring and in life. For more emphasis on this point, read the next story about a young boxer named Gordon.

Gordon was a talented young boxer with raw skill and potential running through his veins. From the moment he walked into the gym, tales of his inherent ability rang off the walls, startling seasoned trainers and fighters alike.

Despite his athletic abilities, Gordon was constantly battling his own psyche. Self-doubt crept into his mind like a shadow, casting doubt on his talents and undermining his confidence day by day. Gordon couldn't ignore the nagging voice in his brain that told him he wasn't good enough, no matter how hard he trained or how many victories he had in the ring.

As he sparred with opponents and hammered the heavy bag with ferocity, Gordon couldn't shake the notion that he was an imposter: a pretender in a sport that required nothing less than authenticity and tenacity. His inner demons murmured tales of failure and inadequacy, sowing seeds of doubt that threatened to choke out life.

But Gordon understood deep down that his troubles were not a reflection of his ability, but rather of his own doubts and concerns. He had the aptitude, energy, and determination to achieve, but the war within his head threatened to destroy his trip before it even began. Despite the darkness that threatened to devour him, Gordon refused to give in to his inner demons.

With each punch thrown, round sparred, and session complete, he faced his concerns head-on, refusing to let self-doubt rule his life. In the process, Gordon discovered a strength within himself that surpassed the physical: the strength of the human spirit, indomitable in the face of hardship and unbreakable in its pursuit of greatness. Because Gordon never gave up, he started to see positive results and only then he felt as if overcoming his self-doubt was achievable, each time he achieved a small win he wrote it down and celebrated it, eventually these wins became consistent and he had multiple pieces of evidence that proved he was a talented young boxer.

Gordon's tale serves as a reminder that success in boxing—and in life—is about mental toughness and resilience in the face of adversity, as much as physical ability. As you continue to investigate the psychological hurdles that stand between you and your potential for greatness, you need to be inspired by Gordon's narrative and find the bravery to fight your own inner demons with conviction, knowing that victory is on the other side of your anxieties.

Imposter Syndrome in Boxing

Imposter syndrome is a psychological phenomenon characterized by feelings of inadequacy, self-doubt, and an ongoing worry of being exposed as a hoax, despite evidence of one's successes and abilities. Those suffering from imposter syndrome sometimes blame their triumphs on chance or external causes, rather than recognizing their own abilities and skills.

Imposter syndrome can take several forms in boxing. A boxer, for example, may mistrust their abilities despite their success in the ring, blaming their victories on luck rather than acknowledging their own hard work and skill. They may feel undeserving of their achievements, thinking that they will be exposed as a fraud if they fail to meet expectations in future bouts. This can cause a lack of confidence, hesitation in the ring, and a reluctance to fully commit to their training and preparation.

Imposter syndrome can also be aggravated by boxing's competitive character and constant pressure to perform well. Boxers may compare themselves to their counterparts, feeling inferior and unsure whether they genuinely belong in the sport. This can lead to a loop of self-doubt and anxiety, limiting their capacity to attain their full potential and appreciate their accomplishments.

Imposter syndrome can be a big barrier to your boxing success because it weakens your confidence, self-belief, and ability to perform to your full potential. By understanding the indicators of impostor syndrome and making efforts to confront and overcome it, you can create a higher feeling of self-assurance, resilience, and authenticity, allowing you to fully enjoy and achieve your talents and pursue your goals with confidence and conviction.

Typical Triggers for Self-Doubt in Boxing

In the tough and demanding world of boxing, there are numerous typical triggers that can cause you to experience worry and self-doubt. Understanding these triggers is critical for you to maintain your mental health and perform at your peak. Here are some common causes of nervousness and self-doubt in boxing:

- **Fear of failure**: Fear of failing is a common cause of anxiety in boxing. You may be concerned about disappointing yourself, your coaches, or your supporters if you don't perform to a particular standard. This worry can put pressure on you to succeed and lead to feelings of inadequacy if expectations are not reached.

- **Comparison to others**: Boxers frequently compare themselves to their peers and competitors, particularly in a highly competitive sport like boxing. Constantly comparing yourself to others can cause feelings of inadequacy and self-doubt, especially if you believe you are falling short in comparison.

- **Performance anxiety**: Whether in training or competition, the pressure to give a great performance in front of an audience can lead to emotions of nervousness and self-doubt. Your confidence and capacity to concentrate on your performance may be affected by worries about making mistakes, doing poorly, or receiving negative feedback from others.

- **Injury and pain**: Boxing has strenuous physical requirements, and there is always a chance of getting hurt. Anxiety over getting harmed or making pre-existing problems worse might affect your confidence and willingness to give your all during training and competition.

- **Uncertainty and unpredictability**: In boxing, there are a lot of uncontrollable factors that can affect the outcome, making it a very unpredictable sport. This ambiguity might make you feel anxious about the future and doubt your capacity to meet any obstacles that may come up in the ring.

- **Pressure from external expectations**: You could experience pressure from sponsors, trainers, or fans to meet and surpass external standards. This strain can be too much to handle, and if you feel that you aren't living up to the expectation, it can make you doubt yourself.

Recognizing these prevalent factors for anxiety and self-doubt in boxing allows you to develop coping techniques and lessen these obstacles. Whether through mental training, relaxing techniques, or seeking support from coaches and colleagues, you must prioritize your mental health and resilience in the face of adversity.

Anxiety and self-doubt in boxing, as in life, are frequently caused by deeply ingrained ideas and cultural expectations that you have of yourself and your talents. These notions can influence how you perceive yourself, your performance, and role in the world of boxing. Below are some typical misconceptions that might lead to worry and self-doubt in life as well as in boxing.

A lot of people including boxers could have unrealistic expectations of themselves and think that they have to perform flawlessly every time in order to be successful. When performance doesn't live up to these irrational expectations, this notion can cause severe pressure to avoid mistakes and feelings of inadequacy.

Due to the heavy emphasis society places on performance and success, many individuals mistake failure for personal inadequacies or worthlessness. For instance, as a boxer, you may fret that losing in the ring might diminish your confidence in your fighting abilities and self-worth.

Being in a sport historically linked with masculinity and toughness may make you feel pressured to conform to stereotypes of what it means to be a "real man." This can include views that men must always be strong, stoic, and in control, which can lead to a reluctance to express vulnerability or acknowledge feelings of uneasiness.

You may be concerned about how you will be seen by others, both within and outside the boxing community. You might be timid of being viewed as weak or incompetent if you make mistakes or show evidence of weakness, so you are hesitant to take risks or go outside of your comfort zone.

Negative self-talk can be a result of internalized ideas about your value and aptitude; and you often engage in critical self-analysis and self-doubt. It might be challenging to give your best effort during training and competition when you are going through this negative internal monologue that saps confidence and self-belief.

Root Causes of Poor Self-Esteem

Nobody is born feeling worthless. You develop poor self-esteem just how you can develop great self-esteem, typically it's the various life experiences and environmental variables that serve as the foundation for how you feel on a day to day basis. It can take months, if not years to fully recover from poor self-esteem, all depending on many factors. Look at a few typical underlying causes and handle them effectively.

Childhood Abandonment Experiences

Children who witness caretakers abandoning or neglecting them may internalize sentiments of inferiority or worthlessness. Deep-rooted convictions that one is undeserving of love and acceptance can result from a lack of constant affection and support. Examples of some famous people who faced childhood abandonment are:

- **Malala Yousafzai**: The Nobel Peace Prize laureate and education activist from Pakistan experienced a form of abandonment when the Taliban targeted her for advocating girls' education.

- **Edgar Allan Poe**: The renowned American writer and poet faced childhood abandonment when his father abandoned the family and his mother died when he was just three years old. Poe was then separated from his siblings and raised by different families, contributing to the sense of isolation and melancholy that often permeated his literary works.

- **Eleanor Roosevelt**: The former First Lady of the United States endured childhood abandonment following the death of her parents at a young age.

- **John Lennon**: The legendary musician and co-founder of The Beatles experienced abandonment by his parents, who separated when he was a child. Lennon's turbulent family life and subsequent emotional struggles influenced his music and activism, shaping his unique artistic expression and worldview.

- **Mother Teresa**: The compassionate nun and missionary faced a different form of abandonment in her childhood, as she witnessed poverty and suffering in her community in Albania. This early exposure to hardship inspired Mother Teresa to dedicate her life to helping the poor and marginalized.

These examples show that not all hope is lost if you have been unfortunate enough to experience childhood abandonment. While you cannot travel back in time and undo the damage, healing from childhood abandonment is possible and requires plenty of healing. It is recommended to attempt the following steps to begin your recovery.

1. **Identify the impact it had.** Write down how you believe the experience has affected your self-worth, relationships, and emotional well-being. Perhaps you find it harder to trust others as you think they may abandon you in a split second, or maybe you feel as if you regulate your emotions poorly as you have had nobody to express your feelings to. Identify the impact, but don't dwell on it too much. Dwelling on past negative emotions for too long can keep these negative thoughts fresh in your mind.
2. **Build self-awareness.** Identify triggers that bring up feelings of abandonment and begin to journal regularly about your emotions to understand yourself better. For example, writing down feelings of frustration and loneliness after being missed out of plans with your so-called friends can help you understand the source of negative emotions.

3. **Develop healthy boundaries.** Learn to say no to things you don't want to do, especially doing favors for friends who don't invite you out for social events. Just because you may annoy these people by rejecting their favors doesn't mean you should put their needs first.
4. **Focus on self-worth.** Become your biggest fan. Do activities that you enjoy, get in shape, stop giving energy to those who leave you out and celebrate these small wins. You will always be the most important person in your life.

Abusive Parents or Caregivers

Being raised in a setting where verbal, emotional, or physical abuse is common can have a significant negative influence on one's sense of self. When parents or other caregivers mistreat their children, the feeling that they are not deserving of love, respect, or happiness may become internalized in the child.

Children raised by abusive parents or caregivers may experience a range of distressing thoughts and emotions that can have lasting effects on their well-being. Such children may constantly fear making mistakes or expressing their true feelings, as they have learned to anticipate punishment or criticism. They may develop a deep sense of shame and worthlessness, believing they deserve the mistreatment they receive. Feelings of confusion and helplessness can also prevail, as the child struggles to understand why they are being subjected to abuse and feels powerless to change their circumstances.

Moreover, these children may internalize the abusive behavior directed towards them, leading to self-blame and a distorted self-image. They might struggle with trust and intimacy in relationships, finding it challenging to form healthy connections due to past betrayals and violations of trust. Additionally, ongoing exposure to abuse can result in feelings of isolation and alienation, as the child may believe they are fundamentally different or unlovable. Coping mechanisms such as dissociation or numbing emotions could develop as a means of self-protection.

Overall, the psychological impact of being raised by abusive parents or caregivers can be complicated, shaping your worldview and emotional well-being in complex ways that may stick with you for the rest of your life if not dealt with. It may be challenging to face the abuse, but if you are somebody who has experienced abuse from parents/caregivers at a young age, attempt the following:

1. **Recognize the abuse.** Whether it was physical, emotional, verbal, or neglect. It's important to remember that the abuse is not your fault, even if the caregiver tries to make you feel responsible.
2. **Transition to independence if you haven't already.** Avoid relying on the abusers for emotional support, financial reasons or otherwise. Even if it requires moving house or finding new employment, this fresh start can be a real boost towards your goal of becoming mentally tough.
3. **Challenge your negative beliefs.** Years of abuse can lead to the negative feelings already discussed. If you feel as if you are unlovable, write down that you are worthy of respect and love, and write down all the reasons why. For example, the achievements you have accomplished, the skills you developed or the activities you enjoy. Reframe the negatives into positives.
4. **Rebuild yourself.** Try new activities, share your story to others, pursue goals, attempt to build new relationships and leave the memories of abuse behind.
5. **Surround yourself with supportive people.** As you rebuild yourself, aim to join communities whether

that be in sports, social events or support groups. You will find people who share a similar upbringing, and you can help uplift each other when times get tough. The boxing gym is always a great community!

Raised With Incorrect Beliefs

Children are highly impressionable, and they frequently adopt the views and attitudes of those around them, particularly authoritative figures like parents, teachers, and peers. If you were reared in an atmosphere in which you were continually fed misinformation or taught harmfully as a child, your internal beliefs are likely to be incorrect, this can cause a great range of issues such as:

- *Difficulty trusting others.*
- *Poor decision-making skills.*
- *Perfectionism.*
- *Having a limited worldview.*
- *Struggling with identity.*
- *Emotional regulation challenges.*

You will be unable to discover whether your internal beliefs are correct or not until you find appropriate education. No matter your current internal beliefs, begin seeking education online from trusted sources for core academic skills, emotional and social skills, general health and well-being, critical thinking and problem solving, finance, life skills, business and creativity. A basic understanding of these topics is a great foundation for building cognitive skills and mental toughness. Reading for 10 minutes a day is a great starter habit to begin developing correct beliefs.

Lack of Positive Role Models

Without good mentors or role models to aspire to, children may find it difficult to establish a strong sense of self-worth. Without someone to support them and believe in their abilities, they could feel lost or undirected, which could result in low self-esteem and feelings of inadequacy.

Children who lack positive role models may face various challenges that can affect their development and well-being. Without healthy examples to emulate, these children may struggle to learn essential life skills, values, and behaviors necessary for success. They may be more susceptible to negative influences from peers, media, or their environment, potentially leading to risky behaviors or poor decision-making.

In the absence of positive role models, children may experience feelings of loneliness, insecurity, and a lack of direction. They may have difficulty setting and achieving goals, as they may not have someone to guide and support them in their endeavors. This can hinder their academic performance, personal growth, and overall sense of self-worth.

Furthermore, the emotional impact of not having positive role models can manifest in issues such as low self-esteem, anxiety, and depression. These children may struggle with forming healthy relationships and may have trust issues due to not having experienced supportive and nurturing connections. So, what should you do if you lacked a positive role model growing up?

Firstly, please note it is never too late to find a good role model, so if you have never had somebody good to look up to, look for:

1. **Somebody who looks for challenges**. Great role models often have overcome many setbacks. Their ability to navigate tough times with grace and determination can be a powerful source of inspiration.
2. **Somebody who is authentic.** A good role model should be someone who is true to themselves and lives in alignment with their beliefs and values, even when it's difficult. Authentic people inspire others to do the same.
3. **Somebody who takes accountability and shows integrity.** Seek someone who takes responsibility for their actions, especially when they are wrong or make a mistake.
4. **Somebody who has commitment to growth.** Find somebody who is curious and continuously seeks to improve himself. By welcoming constructive criticism, they are motivated to become better.

There are many more characteristics to look for but use the above as a great starter. Remember, your role model doesn't have to be perfect because as humans, nobody is perfect. People will always make mistakes; the best role models are those who bounce back from mistakes effectively and avoid repeating them. Examples of good male role models include Muhammad Ali, Steve Irwin and Alex Hormozi.

Traumatic Experiences

Traumatic situations like loss, bullying, or accidents can all have a negative impact on self-esteem. These experiences can undermine a person's sense of safety and security in the world, causing emotions of vulnerability, helplessness, and low self-esteem. Trauma needs to be dealt with, unfortunately I have experienced a close family member develop paranoid schizophrenia because of suppressing trauma for years, therefore I urge you to follow the advice below if you have undealt trauma.

1. **Face the pain.** When faced with trauma, no matter its severity, ensure to acknowledge the hurt. Don't downplay, deny or suppress the feelings that come with trauma as it makes matters worse down the line. Try to understand what happened and express your emotions with journaling, breathing exercises or other activities that help clear your mind.
2. **Seek support.** Share your feelings with a friend, family member, or mentor who can listen without judgment. Keeping feelings of trauma to yourself can lead to feelings of isolation and your emotions can feel overwhelming.

3. **Look for meaning.** Rather than seeing trauma as purely destructive, explore what lessons the trauma has taught you about yourself, others, or life in general. For example, a death in the family can be a wakeup call to have greater appreciation for the life of your loved ones.
4. **Look for growth.** Try to reframe it as an experience that has contributed to your growth. Ask yourself how the trauma has changed you and what strengths you've developed as a result. Ask yourself, "How can I use this experience to become stronger, wiser, or more empathetic?" Furthermore, take this opportunity to build new healthy habits.
5. **Life goes on.** Traumatic events happen to people all the time, accept the harsh reality of life and be prepared for when your next bad day awaits. Having dealt with trauma in the past you may feel more confident in your ability to handle it in the future.

Comparison to Others

Low self-esteem can also result from feeling inadequate and constantly comparing oneself to others. People who believe they fall short of others' accomplishments or society's expectations may feel inadequate in a society that frequently places a high importance on outward appearance and success.

Comparing a child to others can have detrimental effects on their self-esteem, confidence, and overall well-being. Constant comparisons can lead to feelings of inadequacy, insecurity, and a sense of never measuring up to perceived standards set by others. Children may internalize these comparisons and develop a negative self-image, believing they are not good enough or worthy of acceptance.

Moreover, comparing a child to their peers can create unhealthy competition and foster a mindset of jealousy or resentment towards others. This can strain relationships and hinder the development of empathy and collaboration skills. Children may also feel pressure to conform to unrealistic expectations, leading to stress, anxiety, and a fear of failure.

Being compared to others as a child usually results in you building a habit of comparing yourself to others in your adult years, and even if you weren't subjected to this as a kid it is very likely you compare yourself to others today. Social media is the driving force behind comparison because it has never been easier to see the best moments of other people's lives. Naturally we compare our current situation to people's best moments, and it can make you think you aren't living your best life.

While some comparisons can be beneficial, for example using other people's achievements for motivation to become better, comparison to others is usually harmful. You may start to wish for the lives of other people; you begin to think your achievements aren't as impressive as you first imagined and may even start to live your life differently to put on a show for others. Remember, your story is completely different to everybody else's therefore it is impossible to have a fair comparison with others. To avoid comparison to others, do the following:

1. **Limit social media use.** Spend less time on social media as this is where most unhealthy comparisons happen. Unfollow accounts or people who make you feel inadequate and follow those that inspire or uplift

you. Use social media blockers to help you. Finally, question whether social media benefits you, I am sure many people would be better off without it.

2. **Set personal goals.** Identify what success means to you rather than adopting societies or others' standards. Measure your progress based on your own goals and milestones, not someone else's achievements. Break down large goals into small steps and reward yourself appropriately for small wins.

3. **Focus on yourself.** You are your own person, while you can show appreciation for other people's achievements, they haven't been through what you've been through. Start comparing yourself to your past self instead of others, are you doing better now than you were 3 months ago?

How to Resolve Low Self-Esteem

Resolving low self-esteem frequently calls for a trifecta of introspection, counseling, and outside assistance. You can start to develop a more resilient and positive sense of self-worth by figuring out the underlying causes of poor self-esteem and challenging and reframing negative ideas. The previous subchapter helped you handle and acknowledge your root causes of poor self-esteem, but to resolve your low self-esteem it takes consistent practice of the following:

- **Regular self-reflection with acknowledgement of the root cause.** The easiest way to do this is to keep a journal, note down parts of the day your self-esteem was low and link them to the root causes. For example, if you are belittled by somebody and couldn't find the strength to stand up for yourself, note it down, link it back to the incorrect beliefs you had as a child and plan to stick up for yourself next time it happens. Eventually as you do this enough, you build a habit of not letting people disrespect you which in turn makes you feel better about yourself.

- **Set realistic goals.** Break down your boxing or life goals into tiny, manageable actions. Concentrate on making gradual improvements rather than striving for perfection. Celebrate each milestone along the way to boost your confidence and momentum. Instead of setting a goal to become a professional boxer straight off the bat, start by setting a goal of completing 2 boxing sessions a week. From this you can continue to set yourself more challenging goals.

- **Act.** Boxers don't improve their boxing skills by thinking about training, they go to every session no matter how they feel and perform to the best of their ability. The point is, if you suffer with low self-esteem, please understand that nobody is going to sprinkle magic dust over you and turn you into a confident individual overnight. You need to keep busy. Build habits of reading, exercising, going to social clubs, and try new things.

- **Practice visualization.** Imagine yourself as a better version of yourself, perhaps in boxing imagine yourself competing and training with self-assurance and success. Moving away from boxing you could picture yourself sticking to a healthy routine, maintaining healthy relationships or enjoying the daily challenges you face. By practicing visualization, you gain emotional insights in what it will feel like to be a better version of yourself, this naturally encourages you to take action to become better.

- **Develop a growth mindset.** Accept the idea that trials and setbacks are chances for growth and learning. Instead of viewing mistakes as failures, consider them useful input that will help you progress and become a better boxer. If you keep punching short of your opponent when sparring, instead of getting angry, take time to review what went wrong, whether that be poor footwork or punching technique and aim to correct it for next time.

- **Focus on the process.** Focus on the process of training and improvement rather than the outcomes and results. Concentrate on understanding the foundations, improving your methods, and giving your all in each training session. Instead of thinking about winning the fight, think about all your next steps in order to get there like your future training sessions, sticking to your healthy diet and how you are going to recover properly after each session.

- **Practice mindfulness**. Integrate mindfulness practices like deep breathing, meditation, or body scans into your workout regimen. Mindfulness can assist to relax the mind, relieve tension and anxiety, and improve attention and concentration.

- **Speak to people.** Sharing your emotions with others doesn't make you weak, it takes plenty of the stress away from you and you are likely to build more meaningful relationships with others doing so. Bottling up your emotions makes matters worse, furthermore your loved ones will get frustrated with you if you don't cough up, trust me people can sense when you're struggling no matter how much you try to hide it. Never hesitate to ask for help from teammates, coaches, or mental health specialists.

- **Forgive / let go.** You cannot hold grudges forever, even Liam Gallagher and Noel Gallagher managed to make up after years of conflict. Allowing conflict to stay unresolved just piles on the stress for both people, and if you can't work something out then just let the relationship go!

- **Become your role model.** If you really have nobody around you to look up to, then become the person that you would look up to. Not as simple as it sounds, however a great question to remind yourself before making each decision is: *would your role model act that way?* For me, I ask myself that question each time I consider cheating on my diet or missing a boxing session.

- **Learn from failure**: Failure is a normal part of the boxing learning curve. Instead of obsessing over mistakes or setbacks, turn them into opportunities to examine what went wrong, discover areas for development, and emerge stronger and more resilient. Again, put pen to paper with this one to give yourself a clear plan to learn from failure.

- **Stay present**: During training and competition, keep your focus on the present moment rather than lingering on past failures or worrying about future outcomes. Stay focused on the present moment and trust in your training and preparedness to get you through. To break the habit of dwelling on past negative emotions, get into the habit of completing 5 pushups every time you find yourself dwelling on past negative thoughts, hopefully this helps you take control of your thoughts.

By applying these techniques and strategies, you may build the mental resilience and confidence required to overcome low self-esteem and self-doubt to perform at your peak in the boxing ring and many other areas of life. While I aim to help you build mental toughness to improve your boxing performance, the real goal is to help you understand and effectively manage your emotions. A strong boxer is nothing without a strong mind.

Stepping outside of your comfort zone is more than testing your physical limits when exercising; it's also about stretching the boundaries of your mental and emotional resilience. When you leave your comfort zone, you face your anxieties and self-doubts, allowing you to develop confidence, resilience, and mental fortitude.

In the sport of boxing, leaving your comfort zone entails pushing yourself to confront new opponents, attempt new training techniques, and compete in unusual locations. It entails accepting the sport's instability and unpredictability while recognizing that growth and improvement are just beyond your anxieties. Outside of boxing you can push yourself even further by facing any personal fears you have such as rejection, failure, heights and the unknown.

So, if you're fighting a battle with your own mind, trying to overcome worry, self-doubt, or limiting beliefs, remember that the greatest way to win is to get out of your comfort zone. Accept the discomfort and the challenge and believe in your ability to rise to the occasion and emerge stronger, more resilient, and more confident than ever before.

Harsh Facts About Negativity

Negativity is a disease in your life and to fight it, here are some hard-hitting truths that you need to learn starting with acknowledgement of your inner voice. The voice in your head is the hardest critic you will ever meet. Though it's simple to fall victim to self-doubt and self-criticism, keep in mind that no one values you more than you do. Don't allow self-deprecating ideas and opinions to prevent you from accomplishing your objectives.

While obstacles and losses are common, wallowing in self-pity will not help the situation. Instead of constantly dwelling on what went wrong, consider how you can move past challenges and become stronger when tackling the adversities of life.

In life, as in boxing, hard work and determination are necessary for success in any pursuit. By wishing for change or just thinking about it, you won't get better. Put in the work, practice regularly, and observe your own development as time goes on. Success rarely comes with a simple or clear route. Expect to encounter challenges and difficulties along the path, whether you're pushing yourself to new heights, conquering hurdles, or pursuing your aspirations.

Accept the difficulty and have faith that the efforts will be repaid. Your thoughts and internal monologue have the power to be either your strongest ally or worst enemy. How can you hope to overcome obstacles outside of yourself if you are unable to overcome your own doubts and fears?

As this chapter comes to an end, it's important to consider the challenging realities you've encountered and their significant implications for success and personal development. Every reality, from facing your inner demons to stepping beyond your comfort zone, is a potent reminder of the mental toughness, tenacity, and perseverance needed to succeed in the boxing world and beyond.

You now know that your worst enemies can be self-doubt and negative self-talk, which weakens your self-esteem and prevents you from realizing your full potential. However, you may start to knock down the obstacles that stand in your way by realizing that you are your own greatest enemy and questioning the veracity of your inner critic.

Keep these harsh realities in mind as you proceed with your path both inside and outside of the ring, and allow them to be a source of empowerment, inspiration, and drive. Accept the difficulties, face your worries, and have faith in your capacity to get past any barriers you may encounter. Because it is through hardship and adversity that you develop.

3. Pursuing Results

Life happens en-route to your objectives, not upon arrival. – Alex Hormozi

In your exploration of the boxing mentality, you've faced the demons of self-doubt and accepted the difficulty of leaving your comfort zone. According to Alex Hormozi, sentiments in the quotation above, emphasis is on the significance of the journey itself, including the daily grind, the habits you develop, and the mindset you acquire along the way.

In this chapter, you will look at how habits may affect your actions as well as your identities. You'll look at the concept of trusting the process, acknowledging that focusing entirely on results can lead to anger and disappointment. Instead, you are encouraged to adopt the process and commit to the daily routine of training, knowing that victory will follow when the process is applied cautiously.

Furthermore, you'll learn about how behaviors impact your self-perception. Consistently engaging in beneficial behaviors, such as frequent training sessions, not only enhances your abilities but also strengthens your identity as a passionate sportsman.

Conversely, half-hearted or intermittent attempts might erase your confidence and retard your growth. A growth mindset is essential for accepting the process and forming habits that result in success. You'll look at how to adopt this mindset, viewing training and drawbacks as possibilities for growth and learning.

To achieve substantial results, prioritize enhancing performance through small, consistent improvements in sleep, diet, exercise, rest, visualization, journaling, and other positive habits. By focusing on these daily routines, you can effectively reach your goals and boost your overall well-being, highlighting the transformative power of incremental changes for success.

Setbacks are unavoidable on the path to success, but they can also offer great learning opportunities. You'll learn how to deal with failures and build resilience, so you can emerge stronger and more motivated than before.

Trust The Process

The secret to success in boxing and life is to have faith in the process. The following are some problems with concentrating only on objectives and the reasons why the process should come first:

- **Outcome dependence**: You get unduly tied to the outcome when you only focus on reaching certain goals, such as winning a fight. This can cause stress, worry, and a fear of failing, all of which can impair your performance. A good example is getting so consumed with winning a boxing match that your concentration and confidence are diminished by your dread of losing.

- **Short-term thinking**: When you are overly devoted to the result, you lose sight of other significant goals, such as winning a battle. This can trigger aspects such as apprehension, tension, and a fear of failing, all of which can deter your capacity to perform. For instance, focusing solely on meeting this week's sales target at the expense of building long-term customer relationships may lead to missed opportunities for customer retention and sustained business growth.

- **External validation**: Seeking approval from others, such as coaches, peers, or fans, might erode your self-esteem and confidence. By focusing on external achievements, you delegate your sense of worth to others rather than establishing a solid foundation of self-belief and self-esteem. Constantly seeking likes and validation on social media can lead to a cycle of comparison, self-doubt, and anxiety, ultimately impacting your mental well-being and sense of self-worth.

Rather than focusing solely on outcomes, it is critical to emphasize the training and improvement process. Regular boxing training, improving your skills, and focusing on continual improvement enables you to lay a firm basis for success. By committing to the process, you may build the discipline, resilience, and mental fortitude required to defeat obstacles while achieving your long-term goals.

Shaping Your Identity

In boxing, as in life, the processes you use and the habits you form play an important role in defining your identity. It is commonly stated that *you are what you repeatedly do*. This ideology emphasizes the significance of consistent, dedicated practice in determining who you are and what you will become. When you commit to training every day and follow a strict training routine, you start to consider yourself as a dedicated and serious boxer.

This consistency not only improves your physical talents and conditioning, but it also strengthens your self-esteem and identity as a dedicated athlete. When your identity is entangled with what you do; you start to identify as someone who is self-disciplined, tough, and committed to lifelong learning.

Think about two boxers: One who practices meticulously every day, following a set regimen, and the other who trains when they feel like it. Through constant effort, the first boxer establishes a solid foundation of abilities, stamina, and mental fortitude. This fighter begins to accept his identity as a serious athlete. They gain confidence from their determination, knowing that they have put in the effort required to succeed.

However, because of his erratic training schedule, the second fighter finds it difficult to develop the same degree of conditioning and expertise. Their irregular endeavors demonstrate a deficiency in dedication, and they could start to perceive themselves as less competent or sincere about the activity. Self-doubt, low self-esteem, and a weakened sense of self as a boxer might result from this inconsistency. Their confidence and performance may be further impacted by others' perception that they are less committed.

Your opinion of yourself is greatly influenced by the procedures you apply. You start to view yourself through the prism of your deeds when you participate in consistent, focused training. Your sense of self becomes more solidified the more you stick to your habits. There is more to this metamorphosis than the superficial adjustments you undergo and this includes aspects concerned with the mental and emotional growth that accompanies consistent effort.

When you train consistently at a high level, you start to exhibit the characteristics of a successful boxer. You gain self-control, resiliency, and a solid work ethic. These characteristics become essential components of your identity, impacting not only your self-perception but also your approach to situations both inside and outside of the ring.

This healthy cycle of development and progress is fueled by good self-perception, which encourages further commitment and persistence.

On the other hand, exercising just when you feel like it results in a disjointed and unstable sense of who you are. Your subconscious becomes confused by sporadic effort and begins to doubt your dedication and ability. This discrepancy may make you feel inadequate and undermine your confidence. Without the strong foundation that comes from regular practice, you can find it more difficult to persevere through obstacles and maintain motivation when they arise.

Coaches, peers, and competitors are more likely to respect and encourage a fighter who consistently performs well. This external affirmation supports your confidence and identity as a dedicated athlete. In contrast, a boxer who practices half-heartedly may struggle to earn the same amount of respect and support, reducing their confidence and motivation.

The Boxing Mentality

It's critical to concentrate on the procedures and routines that characterize your everyday life if you want to develop a strong boxer personality. The following are some crucial tactics:

- **Establish a timetable**: Create and adhere to a regular training regimen. Building mental toughness and physical skills both require consistency. Committing to a daily routine can enhance your creativity and productivity over time, as consistent practice hones your skills and mental discipline. Routines don't have to be complicated, for example starting each day with a short walk/run and setting yourself a regular bedtime is a great starting point.

- **Put quality first**: Pay attention to how well your training sessions go. Not only must you show up, but you must also always give it your all. Begin tracking your training sessions, journal the mistakes you made and how you can correct them next time, note down how much effort you put in and record how often you felt demotivated or low on energy. Style your training journal however you think works best, as long as you form that habit of reviewing each session it is likely to set you up for continuous improvement.

- **Look the part:** How could you possibly feel like a competent boxer if you don't look like one? Purchase good boxing gear, get in fantastic shape, end each session soaking in sweat and act like you're the most confident person in every room you walk into. Just because you don't look the part yet doesn't mean you can't work towards it. A big emphasis on good boxing gear, if you truly want to stick with boxing then invest in quality gear, not only will your body appreciate it but financially it will motivate you to train harder.

- **Think and modify**: Evaluate your progress on a regular basis and modify your training plan as needed. This keeps you motivated and involved. Regularly reviewing your fitness regimen, tracking your performance, and adjusting your workout plan based on your progress and goals ensures that you stay engaged and motivated to achieve optimal results.

You may change who you are and see yourself as a committed, strong, and talented boxer by putting these strategies into practice. Your ability to overcome obstacles, maintain motivation, and accomplish your goals in the ring and in life will be bolstered by this strong sense of self.

Develop A Growth Mindset

A growth mindset, promoted by psychologist Carol Dweck, is the view that skills and intelligence can be developed through dedication, hard work, and perseverance. This differs from a fixed mindset, in which people feel their abilities and intelligence are static and immutable. In boxing, developing a growth mindset is critical for ongoing improvement, resilience, and long-term success.

The idea of a growth mindset is based on the fact that obstacles and setbacks provide opportunities for learning and improvement. When you have a growth mindset you regard failure as a stepping stone to mastery, rather than a reflection of your talents. This viewpoint pushes you to accept challenges, persevere in the face of adversity, and constantly look for opportunities to develop.

Why a Growth Mindset Is Essential in Boxing

A growth mindset is beneficial in many areas in life because as it suggests, it is a state of mind that encourages growth in whichever area of life you are pursuing goals in. As already discussed, boxing is a tough discipline therefore requires much more effort to grow as a fighter, below are a few reasons exactly why you must develop a growth mindset for boxing.

- **Overcoming challenges**: Boxing is a sport that presents constant challenges, such as demanding training regimens and tough opponents. Fighters with a growth mentality can see these challenges as opportunities to grow and learn rather than insurmountable barriers. Therefore, a growth mindset would encourage fighters, who feel as if their boxing sessions don't challenge them physically or mentally enough, to make adjustments to their training regimen.

- **Resilience**: The game of boxing is both cerebral and physical. Athletes who have a growth attitude are more resilient; they can bounce back from drawbacks and turn them into chances to get better. It is hard to find any professional boxers who give up easily, that's for sure.

- **Constant improvement**: Fighters who never stop trying to get better eventually become the best. A growth mindset offers a passion for education and the drive to become proficient in novel abilities and behaviors.

How to Acquire a Growth Mindset in Boxing

Many people are content with just about getting by in life, they are un-bothered about whether their name gets heard, whether they achieve their goals and don't care about the bigger picture. I struggle to comprehend that mindset as I find that without the drive for growth, then what really is the point of doing anything?

But I haven't always had this growth mindset, boxing is what gave me the mindset to want to achieve more, before boxing I thought I was happy to work a boring job, eat plenty of junk food and spend my spare time escaping reality with video games and other forms of instant gratification. The truth is that I was lost and many people are too, so while boxing helps you develop a growth mindset, here's more advice on how to acquire it.

- **Embrace challenges**: Consistently push yourself past your comfort zone. Venturing beyond your comfort zone is crucial for personal development, whether it's attempting a novel project, engaging in sparring with a more proficient opponent, or intensifying your exercise regimen. Criticism that is constructive is priceless. Accept judgment from coaches, peers, and even yourself without reservation. Utilize it to pinpoint problem areas and implement the required fixes. When I was much younger I always shied away from challenges because I feared the possibility of embarrassment if I failed, however looking back now I wish I had challenged myself much more often because my best learning experiences have come from times I've failed miserably at something. Even though embarrassment is hard to stomach, it seriously helps you understand where you went wrong and prevents you from repeating similar mistakes.

- **Learn from your mistakes**: View setbacks and errors as teaching moments rather than as failures. Examine what went wrong, determine why it occurred, and come up with fixes to prevent such errors in the future. Acknowledge that failure is a necessary component of learning. Triumph over hardship by realizing that every obstacle you face brings you one step closer to your objectives. For example, if you keep dropping your hands after throwing a punch, ask your partner to throw a light punch at your head just after you throw a punch, this way you are much more likely to build that muscle memory as there's a potential for you to be harmed. Simple corrective drills like that quickly iron out errors.

- **Cultivate a love for learning**: Always be eager to acquire new boxing techniques, strategies, and expertise. This inquisitiveness will fuel ongoing progress and keep you invested in the sport. Set learning and skill development goals rather than performance goals. Concentrate on learning a new method or grasping the nuances of a specific plan. An easy habit to encourage learning is to start reading various self-help books for 10 minutes each day.

- **Adopt positive self-talk**: Replace negative thoughts with positive affirmations. Remind yourself that effort leads to improvement and that every boxer, even the greats, started from a place of not knowing. Instead of swearing at yourself for missing multiple punches in a sparring session, accept the loss in the moment and task yourself to land more punches in your next session. Even if you land just one more punch, you have made progress and you can dwell on that as a positive rather than a negative. Also, try to focus on the positives from that session, just because you missed a few punches shouldn't ruin the effort you put in for the entire session.

- **Focus on effort, not outcome**: Praise yourself for your efforts rather than the results. Recognize your hard work and attention to your training, regardless of the immediate outcome. Although having the long term goal in your head can be quite motivating, as you get months into training it is much more effective to focus on the present. Are you performing as well as you can in each session? Are you sticking to a healthy diet? How are you going to recover after your session?

Building a Supportive Environment

Our environment is everything surrounding us that supports and influences our lives. Whether that's the people you spend the most time with, your living area, the technology you use and other variables that influence you, you must ensure that your environment supports you as much as possible to aid you achieve your goals.

- **Find growth-oriented peers**. Training with others who share a growth mindset can be beneficial as their positive attitude and approach can serve as a source of inspiration and motivation, establishing your own determination to improve and develop. Joining local meet-up groups, online communities, or networking events focused on personal or professional development can help you connect with like-minded individuals who share a growth mindset, providing you with a supportive environment for learning and growth.

- **Seek mentors**. Find mentors and coaches that place a strong emphasis on development and learning. Throughout your life, their advice and assistance will be invaluable. Seek out mentors and coaches in your field of interest through networking events, professional organizations, or online platforms like LinkedIn, reaching out to them with a clear request for guidance and demonstrating your eagerness to learn.

- **Optimize your living area.** You probably spend most of your time at home, therefore set it up in a way that influences you to work towards your goals. If you struggle to get good sleep every night, think about taking electronic devices and other distractions out of your bedroom. If you can't always make it to the boxing gym, set up a small area for boxing practice in your house.

Small Changes, Significant Results

It's simple to get caught up in the big picture when striving for boxing excellence: taking home titles, perfecting cutting-edge methods, or reaching peak physical fitness. But the little behaviors that add up over time are the cornerstone of any major accomplishment. When these behaviors are consistently followed, major outcomes and long-term success are achieved.

The fundamentals of performance are habits. They mold your daily schedules, impact your actions, and ultimately decide your level of success. Developing excellent habits can mean the difference between an average and an outstanding boxing performance. You can provide a strong basis for ongoing improvement by concentrating on modest, doable adjustments.

Athletes in general need adequate sleep, but boxers in particular require it because of their high levels of physical and mental stress. Muscles repair, the body heals itself, and the mind takes in and sorts new information as we sleep. Every night, try to get seven to nine hours of quality sleep. Make a routine for yourself that includes engaging in calming activities, avoiding devices for an hour before bed, and maintaining a regular sleep pattern (going to sleep at the same time daily). You will eventually perform better, react quicker, and heal from injuries more rapidly if you receive more quality sleep. Your bed should only be used for having sex and sleeping, therefore stop watching TV or using your phone in bed. As your brain associates activities with its environment, your brain prepares you to do these activities when you get into bed - making it harder for you to sleep.

The way an athlete eats affects their performance greatly. Eating a healthy diet guarantees that your body has the fuel it needs to perform and recover. Start by modifying your diet in one or two areas. This could involve eating more veggies, consuming more lean proteins, or consuming fewer sugar-filled snacks and beverages. Your body will receive the nourishment it requires for maximum performance and recuperation from these minor adjustments.

As vital as hard training sessions are, the real driver of improvement in any fitness plan is consistency. Better physical conditioning and skill acquisition result from consistent, concentrated practice. Make a training plan that is both attainable and long-term. Make the commitment to consistent, concentrated sessions rather than sometimes pushing yourself to the edge. For instance, if you're currently training twice a week, try adding a short, additional session focusing on a specific skill or conditioning drill. The consistency will pay off more than occasional, intense bursts of training. Furthermore, when starting your training don't make it too difficult right off the bat, start small and work your way up as it reduces the likelihood of you giving up when it feels too challenging.

Recuperation and rest are just as crucial as the actual workout. Both your body and mind cannot function at their peak without enough sleep. Make time in your calendar for active recuperation and rest days. Pay attention to your body and give it time to heal. Stretching, yoga, or gentle aerobic exercises can help you heal while keeping you moving during rest days.

Small adjustments have the advantage of being sustainable and manageable. Even though a single tiny adjustment might not seem like much, when added up over time, these minor adjustments result in considerable advancements. This idea, often known as the "compound effect," proposes that daily improvements we make consistently can have a significant impact over an extended period of time.

Think about this: over the course of a year, even a 1% increment per day will add up to a big improvement, 37 times better to be exact. Substantial improvements in performance, abilities, and general well-being result from this gradual progress.

Establish simple, useful behaviors first. Concentrate on one habit at a time. Making too many changes at once can be exhausting and unworkable. Choose one area to work on, like your food or sleep patterns, and make a tiny, targeted adjustment there. For example, a small habit to aid sleep would be to not use technology after 9pm. To establish new habits, you must be consistent. To make your new habit a seamless part of your daily routine, give it your whole attention for at least 30 days. Let's be real, life is full of unexpected events and it is very easy to let a habit slip for one day, this is never a problem, just always aim to never let it slip to two consecutive days, as then it becomes repetition!

It is advisable to monitor your development as a person. To track your progress, utilize an app or a notebook. Observing your progress, no matter how tiny, may be immensely inspiring. Remain adaptable and flexible when necessary, but always try to get back on track as quickly as you can.

In boxing, as in life, little, consistent improvements can have a big impact. You can lay a solid foundation for success by focusing on healthy habits such as sleep, food, exercise, and rest. Recall that greatness is not acquired overnight, but rather by consistent, continuous effort to improve every day. Believe in the power of tiny changes and let them lead you to your ultimate goals.

Managing Setbacks

Setting yourself back on the path to becoming a great boxer is unavoidable. Every athlete has obstacles that put their willpower to the test, whether it is a difficult defeat, an injury, or a dip in performance. It's critical to realize that obstacles are a necessary component of development and growth. The secret is to learn how to deal with these challenges, not to avoid them.

First and foremost, it's critical to understand that failures do not define you. Although they are transient, they offer worthwhile educational opportunities. When anything goes wrong, step back and assess what caused the setback. Was your training plan too difficult? Are you getting enough quality sleep? Is your diet poor? Are there things on your mind distracting you? Recognizing the underlying reason will enable you to fix the issue and stop it from nagging you.

Keeping an optimistic outlook is one strategy for handling failures well. This doesn't imply denying the situation's reality; rather, it suggests concentrating on your controllable circumstances and areas for improvement. Positive self-talk has a lot of power. Remind yourself of your accomplishments in the past, your strengths, and your capacity to overcome obstacles. This change in viewpoint might help you stay inspired and goal-focused. Setting reasonable expectations is another essential component in handling setbacks. Recognize that, like other sports, boxing advancement is not linear. There'll be high points and low points. When things don't go according to plan, accepting this fact might help you maintain your resilience. Enjoy the little successes and accomplishments along the road; they can help you feel more optimistic and keep you moving forward.

Furthermore, it might be quite beneficial to have a solid support system. Be in the company of people who support you and your objectives. You can stay motivated and grounded by seeking support and comments from your friends, family, coach, or training partners. Talk to them about your troubles and ask for guidance without holding back. Occasionally, an external viewpoint can provide valuable perspectives that you might have missed. Establishing a schedule for healing and self-care is also crucial. Rehab and appropriate rest are necessary after physical setbacks like injuries. Activities that enhance mental health and relaxation might help with mental setbacks like burnout or lack of motivation. This could be engaging in other activities besides boxing, practicing meditation, or just taking a break to rejuvenate. I have found walking in the countryside is a great way to deal with stress or setbacks.

Lastly, it's crucial to develop endurance and patience. It takes time to become successful at boxing. It necessitates commitment, diligence, and the capacity to move past setbacks. Accept the road and have faith that every obstacle will ultimately lead you closer to your objective. You may defeat obstacles and grow stronger from every experience if you have realistic expectations, an optimistic outlook, seek help, prioritize self-care, and never stop learning.

Building Resilience

Developing the mental and emotional fortitude required to overcome obstacles is the foundation of building resilience, which is a continuation of handling setbacks. It is possible to develop resilience as a skill through deliberate experiences and practices rather than as an innate quality. Resilience is essential for both life and boxing in order to achieve long-term success and weather the journey's unavoidable highs and lows.

A useful strategy for developing resilience is to make tiny, gradual goals and work toward them. These objectives provide stepping stones and give a feeling of advancement and success. For example, instead of starting off trying to run a marathon, set weekly or daily objectives like running a 10k and build up to it. Reaching these little objectives can boost your self-esteem and provide a positive feedback loop that encourages advancement. Effective emotion management is a crucial component in developing resilience. Emotional rollercoasters associated with win and defeat can occur in boxing. Gaining emotional control abilities can help you remain composed and concentrated under pressure. Examples of these abilities are visualization and deep breathing exercises. You can manage your emotional reactions by maintaining a clear head and making better decisions, both in and out of the ring.

The need for mental and physical resilience is equal. This entails taking good care of your body through appropriate exercise, diet, and relaxation. You can endure the physical demands of boxing and heal from injuries more rapidly if your body is in top shape. Including routines like strength training, regular stretching, and getting enough sleep will improve your overall performance and physical toughness.

Resilience is also developed from experience. You get stronger the more obstacles you meet and overcome. Accept the difficult moments as teaching opportunities that help you become a more resilient person. Use your prior experiences as a source of inspiration and strength by thinking back on your failures and how you overcome them. Knowing that you will become better at defeating challenges surely acts as encouragement to keep challenging yourself?

Finally, keeping a cheerful attitude and practicing appreciation might boost your resilience. Focusing on the positives in your life and being appreciative for your progress, no matter how modest, can help you change your perspective and gain a feeling of purpose and motivation. This positive mindset can help you face challenging situations with optimism and persistence.

As you end this chapter, keep in mind that the path to success in boxing, as in life, is fraught with obstacles, failures, and defeats. Losing successfully means finding value in every event, no matter how difficult or disappointing it may appear at the time. It's about accepting that every failure is a step toward becoming a stronger, more skillful, and determined fighter.

Do not be afraid to take on the most difficult challenges. Instead, seek them out and face them head-on. Taking on challenging opponents, pushing through grueling training sessions, as well as persevering through moments of doubt and fatigue are essential aspirations that you should embrace. Not only will this attitude help you build mental and physical toughness, you will have great stories to tell and memories that will sit with you well for the rest of your life.

Most of the time we need to experience some kind of pain to learn, just how toddlers fall over and graze their knees when learning to walk. You are bound to experience plenty of physical and psychological pain from boxing training, it is a natural part of the learning process so don't get upset when training does get tough. This isn't your call to get beaten up all of the time, but keep in mind that if your training sessions don't feel physically exhausting or mentally challenging you should step it up.

Or you could fail once and give up. You could tell everybody your plans to get into boxing and quit halfway through your first session telling everybody that "circuits have nothing to do with boxing, so what's the point" apparently, when in fact you couldn't keep up with the intensity. When you return home from the first session not having completed the training, would you feel proud to tell everyone that you gave up that easily? Or would you lie? The choice is yours, give up straight away or keep trying, we both know which leads to the better outcome.

4. Enhancing Cognitive Control

You now know that moving forward requires overcoming hurdles and that setbacks are inevitable but manageable. Enhancing cognitive regulation is a crucial skill for you to have, and it will be covered in this chapter.

Cognitive control refers to the mental processes that allow you to regulate your thoughts, feelings, and behaviors in order to achieve your goals. Cognitive control is critical for you to make well-informed judgments, focus, control your emotions, and maintain composure under pressure. By learning about and enhancing your cognitive abilities, you can optimize your potential and enhance your performance in the ring.

In this chapter, you will explore the definition and applications of cognitive control in boxing, as well as its several forms. You will then look at basic strategies to enhance cognitive control, such as emotion recognition and regulation, stress management, mindfulness, concentration, maintaining composure under pressure, and the potency of visualization. You may employ any of these strategies to assist you in developing the mental toughness needed to be successful in the ring and beyond.

The following goals are what this chapter aims to teach you. Provide a thorough explanation of cognitive control and how boxing relates to it. Provide useful advice on how to enhance cognitive control, such as stress management, emotional control, focus, poise under duress, cognitive training activities, mindfulness, and visualization.

The chapter will also give you the tools to apply these tactics in your workouts and competitive matches to help you reach your boxing objectives while improving your performance. Let's examine each of these tactics in more detail and see how they might help you advance and succeed as a boxer.

Understanding Cognitive Control in Boxing

You can effectively regulate your thoughts, emotions, and behaviors to achieve your goals thanks to a group of brain mechanisms called cognitive control. Among other cognitive functions, they encompass inhibition, planning, memory, attention, and problem-solving abilities. Making rapid decisions and maintaining composure under pressure are only two of the many ways in which boxing effectiveness depends on cognitive control.

Types of Cognitive Control

There are various factors of cognitive control, and each one has a distinct purpose in controlling thought and behavior:

- **Inhibition**: To focus on the task at hand, you must be able to resist ideas, urges, or behaviors that are irrelevant or distracting. Inhibition is crucial to boxing because it helps you stay focused and prevent rash or impulsive moves during a bout.

- **Working memory**: The term "working memory" describes the capacity to temporarily store and process information while engaging in cognitive tasks. Working memory is essential to boxing since it allows you to recall and execute complex combos, plan moves throughout a fight, and quickly adjust to shifting circumstances.

- **Attention**: The capacity to block out distractions and selectively focus on pertinent information is known as attentional control. In the sport of boxing, attentional control is essential for keeping an eye on the opponent's movements, responding fast to strikes, and predicting their next move.

- **Flexibility**: Cognitive flexibility refers to the ability to adapt to changing circumstances, switch between tasks or mental sets, and generate alternative solutions to problems. As a boxer, you discover that cognitive flexibility allows you to adjust your tactics and strategies in response to your opponent's movements and counter-strategies.

- **Planning and problem-solving**: To accomplish desired results, these cognitive processes entail creating plans of action, formulating strategies, and establishing goals. Planning and problem-solving abilities are critical in boxing as they are needed to create a combat strategy, assess the opponent's advantages and disadvantages, and make tactical changes throughout the fight.

Importance of Cognitive Control

It is impossible to exaggerate how crucial cognitive control is to boxing. It affects every facet of your game and is a basic component of athletic performance. The following justifies the necessity of cognitive control for boxing success:

- **Decision-making**: Boxing is a dynamic, fast-paced sport where quick decisions are needed. You have to continuously evaluate the moves of your opponent, predict their next move, and select the best counter move. When you possess cognitive control, you make fast, correct decisions under duress, increasing your chances of winning in the ring.

- **Focus and concentration**: To perform well in boxing, you must remain focused and attentive. As a boxer you need to be completely focused on the battle, constantly aware of your surroundings, and sensitive to the movements of your opponent. All it takes is a lapse of concentration for a split second to get knocked out. Athletes who possess cognitive control are better able to block out distractions, maintain focus, and sustain mental toughness throughout a fight.

- **Emotional regulation**: Being an emotionally charged sport, boxing may make you go through a variety of emotions, such as fear, excitement, frustration, and rage. Retaining composure under duress, controlling performance anxiety, and avoiding impetuous or careless actions in the ring all depend on effective emotional management. If you have cognitive control, you are able to control your emotions, remain composed under duress, and give your best work when it counts most. Usually, opponents will try to get under your skin so you need to have great composure to avoid losing control of yourself.

- **Adaptability**: Cognitive control enables you to remain flexible, resilient, and adaptable in the face of adversity, ensuring that you respond effectively to changing circumstances in the ring. Boxing is a dynamic and unpredictable sport where circumstances can change rapidly. You should be able to adapt to unexpected situations, adjust your tactics on the fly, and seize opportunities as they arise. For example, your opponent could drop out two weeks before a fight and you need to prepare for a completely different foe.

Regulating Your Emotions in Boxing

Regulating your emotions is important in boxing because it determines how you perform and make decisions in the ring. You can perform at a higher level if you are able to understand your emotions and develop appropriate coping mechanisms. During training and competition, you frequently feel a wide range of emotions, including anxiety, enthusiasm, fury, and frustration.

Numerous things, like the ferocity of the battle, the pressure to succeed, memories from the past, and interactions with coaches and opponents, might set off these feelings. You can better understand your emotional reactions and create tactics to control them by identifying the particular circumstances or events that set off certain emotions.

You need to be aware of the reasons behind your feelings and how these affect your performance. Anxiety or worry, for instance, might be brought on by pressure to live up to expectations or by fear of failing. Errors or failures in competition or training can be the source of frustration. You might have a greater grasp of your psychological state and how it affects your performance by investigating the underlying causes of your emotions.

You need to also control your emotions and perform at your best when you have identified your emotional triggers and comprehended the causes of their sentiments. When it comes to managing emotions while boxing, deep breathing, visualization, positive self-talk, mindfulness practices, and getting help from coaches or mental health specialists are some useful strategies.

When you are nervous before a bout or at intense moments in the ring you can find relief from tension and anxiety by taking slow, deep breaths. Your confidence and motivation can be increased and feelings of uncertainty or fear can be managed by visualizing success and positive outcomes. You are capable of overcoming negative ideas and attitudes, increasing your confidence, and keeping a positive outlook during practice and competition by employing constructive self-talk.

As a fighter, you can sustain your composure and focus under pressure in the ring by using mindfulness exercises including body scanning, focused breathing, and meditation. It is also possible for you to benefit greatly from the advice and help of coaches, teammates, or mental health specialists in handling challenging emotions and creating useful coping mechanisms.

Finally, never aim to become emotionless or suppress your emotions. Emotions help us connect with others, make decisions, stay motivated, and process experiences. Suppressing your emotions can lead you to a life that feels empty. Instead, put yourself in situations that trigger as many different emotions as possible, this doesn't mean to only do things that trigger negative emotions, but make an attempt to live a life that brings you a balance of happiness, sadness, anger, fear and surprise. The more you become exposed to these emotions the better you can handle them going forward. Any emotion, either positive or negative, can distract you, ruin your sleep and hinder your performance when it matters, therefore, learn to regulate your emotions with gradual exposure.

Concentration Techniques

Your ability to focus is crucial to your performance. Whether in the heat of a contest or during training, the capacity to concentrate completely on the task at hand might mean the difference between success and failure. Gaining focus is essential in boxing since every second counts and even the slightest distraction can result in a knockdown or worse.

In boxing, concentration is the ability to pay close attention to multiple things at once, including the movements of the opponent, your personal technique and plan, the coach's instructions, and the constantly shifting dynamics of the fight. Mental acuity and endurance are necessary for this diverse attention, and they can be improved and increased with the help of particular methods and exercises.

The fast-paced and unpredictable nature of boxing is one of the main reasons focus is essential. You need to anticipate punches, respond swiftly to moves made by your opponent, and grasp opportunities for counterattacks. You need to provide this degree of attentiveness with your complete focus. Any diversion or daydreaming might lead to lost opportunities or, worse, expose you to an attack from an adversary. In order to enhance focus and retention, you might implement various efficacious strategies that involve mindfulness and meditation.

Mindfulness and Meditation

You can significantly increase focus by frequently including mindfulness and meditation activities in your engagements. Being aware means focusing on the now and observing ideas and emotions without making assumptions about them. Those fighters who practice mindfulness can learn to concentrate under pressure and let go of distractions. Two meditation methods that can help quiet the mind and sharpen mental attention are focused breathing and visualization (guided imagery). These methods can help you concentrate during practice and competition. The following details give instructions on how to undertake these two types of meditation.

Focused Breathing

Focused breathing is an astonishing and productive form of meditation that is designed to slow down your breathing rate. In order to perform this practice, draw in sufficient air to fill the space in your lungs, then exhale gradually. In certain moments using your nose to breathe out is simpler because it has a smaller opening that assists in controlling the speed of exhalation. Briefly pause after exhaling and then inhale again.

Another breathing technique that I find useful is box breathing. I have found it useful for calming my mind, reducing stress and improving focus. The best part is that it only takes 5 minutes to complete. Below are the instructions or look for guided box breathing exercises on YouTube.

- Inhale: Slowly inhale through your nose for a count of 4 seconds. Focus on filling your lungs completely with air.
- Hold: Hold your breath for 4 seconds. Try to remain relaxed during this pause.
- Exhale: Slowly exhale through your mouth for a count of 4 seconds. Focus on emptying your lungs completely.
- Hold: Hold your breath again for 4 seconds before starting the next inhale.
- Repeat: You can repeat this cycle for 5 minutes or until you feel calmer and more centered.

Visualization

Visualization is among the best techniques for sharpening attention. You can practice specific motions and scenarios in your mind, which helps you see your performance clearly. When you engage in this mental activity you might become more prepared and focused, which will enable you to execute your strategies more accurately. Furthermore, by preparing the mind for a range of situations, visualization helps to increase confidence. This topic is covered in greater detail later on in this chapter.

Striving for Clear Results

When you establish precise, measurable objectives for every practice and match you are able to sustain your motivation and focus. With a vivid objective in mind, such as perfecting a particular technique or following a predetermined game plan, you are more likely to remain focused on the task at hand. Breaking down more ambitious goals into smaller, more manageable tasks may also make it easier to stay focused and track progress. The next steps will be beneficial in enabling you to achieve this:

1. *Ascertain the necessary steps to achieve the objective.*

2. *Your goal should be divided into high-level subgoals.*

3. *Divide the first sub-goal into manageable chunks.*

4. *Plan when to do the first step.*

5. *Execute, repeat, and adjust as needed.*

Below is an example of how to follow the instructions listed above, of course we will stick to the theme of boxing training. Hopefully, you begin to see just how effective this is for striving toward clear results. Example: The overall objective is to compete in an amateur boxing match within 12 months, with the aim of winning the bout.

Step 1: What must be done to achieve the objective?

In order to compete in an amateur boxing match within 12 months first, I must understand the basics of boxing and my requirements for competing such as the weight class I wish to compete at, learn the rules of boxing, look for quality boxing gear and get a license if required. Next joining a boxing gym is a crucial step, ensuring it has a good reputation and ensuring they train beginners to compete at an amateur level. After joining the gym, I need to stick to a solid routine. This routine should consist of regular boxing training, a healthy diet, regular fitness sessions and take into consideration recovery. As time goes by I can adjust my routine to meet requirements and begin to think about mental preparation and tactics.

Step 2: How can this goal be divided into subgoals?

Subgoal 1: Research and prepare for the first boxing session.

Subgoal 2: Join a boxing gym and build a strong foundation of basic boxing skills.

Subgoal 3: Build and follow a routine that improves fitness, strength, and endurance.

Subgoal 4: Spar and gain ring experience.

Subgoal 5: Prepare for the match.

Step 3: Divide the First Subgoal into Manageable Chunks

First Subgoal: Research and prepare for the first boxing session.

Chunk 1: Research the boxing basics.

Task 1: Search for resources that explain the rules and regulations (weight classes, scoring system, illegal moves and fouls etc.)

Task 2: Search for resources that showcase different boxing training methods (shadowboxing, bag work, circuits, bag work and conditioning etc.)

Task 3: Search for resources that explain the basic boxing techniques (stance, footwork, punching techniques and defensive techniques etc.) for a basic understanding.

Chunk 2: Prepare for the first boxing session.

Task 1: Research local boxing gyms online and read reviews, ensure they teach beginners and have a good reputation.

Task 2: Research and purchase beginner boxing gear (gloves, handwraps, shoes, mouthguard etc.)

Task 3: Research and build a simple training routine to prepare you for your first session (begin regular training such as running, shadowboxing, bodyweight exercises etc.)

To give you a better example, I have included the first 2 subgoals for this example.

Second Subgoal: Join a boxing gym and build a strong foundation of basic boxing skills.

Chunk 1: Fully commit to a boxing gym that allows me to compete at an amateur level.

Task 1: Attend my first session at the boxing gym I've decided is best from prior research.

Task 2: Review my first session *(what did I learn? were the coaches respectful and helpful? was I challenged mentally and physically?)*

Task 3 (optional): Attend a session at other gyms and compare which is best.

Task 4: Commit to the gym and coach that aligns with my needs.

Chunk 2: Begin developing my boxing skills at the gym and continuously practice/ research at home.

Task 1: Focus on proper boxing stance and footwork. Practice daily. Reflect on my boxing sessions and use online resources to help.

Task 2: Learn and practice basic punches (jab, cross, hook, uppercut) with a coach and on the heavy bag. Also regularly practice with shadowboxing and record myself to review my technique.

Task 3: Practice defensive techniques like blocking, slipping, and parrying. Best practice is with a partner.

Chunk 3: Increase Training Frequency

Task 1: Attend boxing classes 2-3 times per week for the first two months.

Task 2: Gradually increase to 4-5 training sessions per week as skills improve.

Task 3: Build a solid routine of boxing training, conditioning, healthy eating, sleeping, recovery and so on.

Step 4: Plan When to Do the First Step

Begin the first step *(research and prepare for the first boxing session)* next week and follow the timeline below.

Week 1

Day 1-2: Research the boxing basics and local boxing gyms online. Begin building a simple routine to prepare for boxing.

Day 3-4: Visit or call 2-3 gyms to inquire about membership and coaching options. Purchase some boxing gear to get started.

Day 5-6: Attend trial classes at two different gyms.

Day 7: Decide and sign up for a membership.

Step 5: Execute, Repeat, and Adjust as Needed

Once I've completed the first step (joining a gym), move on to the next chunk of tasks (developing basic techniques). Track my progress by assessing how well I've mastered basic boxing skills and adjust my training routine as required. *Remember, you don't have to (and wont) get your training plan/routine perfect on the first attempt, it takes plenty of trial and error to find out what works best to help you achieve your goals. It will take months to get in a position where you feel like what you are doing is working.* Below are some basic guidelines.

Month 1-2: Focus on Chunk 2: Regular practice of footwork, basic punches and defensive techniques with feedback from my coach.

Month 3-4: Move to Chunk 3: Increase training frequency to build muscle memory and stamina. Ensure I'm following a strong routine.

Ongoing:

- **Adjust Goals:** As I progress, evaluate how well I am mastering techniques and gaining fitness. I may need to adjust timelines or spend more time on certain aspects before moving forward.
- **Repeat Process:** Continue with each subgoal, breaking them down into smaller, manageable chunks, and executing them step by step.
- **Long-Term Execution:** By the time I reach the end of the 12-month timeline, I should be sparring regularly and preparing mentally and tactically for my amateur boxing match. Continue refining your skills, fitness, and mental toughness to compete confidently.

Although that is a very basic example, I hope it gives you an idea of how you really have to adapt as you go along. As a complete beginner you will seriously struggle to work out how to optimize your training straight away, as you gain experience and speak to other people with similar goals you begin to adjust your program and goals as you progress. Furthermore, as you gain experience you may realize that your initial goal was too easy or completely unachievable in that time frame. If you don't get it right the first time, don't see it as an excuse to give up, reassess and come up with a new plan. Sometimes failure is necessary for bouncing back stronger.

Mental Conditioning Exercises

It has been demonstrated that mental training exercises enhance cognitive skills connected to attention. Playing games, solving puzzles, and using brain-training applications can improve working memory, cognitive flexibility, and attention span. Attempt to complete various brain training exercises each day, perhaps just 5-10 minutes after a meal.

Another way to condition your mind is with emotional regulation drills. In boxing, you must ensure that you can control your emotions under intense pressure or when facing adversity from others. Lacking this control can lead to reckless behavior, a great example of this is when Mike Tyson chewed on Evander Holyfield's ear mid fight. Practice techniques like labeling emotions ("I am feeling angry"), reframing thoughts, or using calming techniques like deep breathing when you feel overwhelmed. Doing this helps you control impulsive reactions, promotes emotional stability, and improves decision-making under pressure.

We also have mental toughness drills, while this book is all about building mental toughness and we have already covered many exercises to help you do so, here is a fitness related mental toughness drill that gets you out of your comfort zone. You could hold difficult positions (like a plank) for extended periods, exercise in challenging conditions (bad weather), or expose yourself to situations where you're out of your comfort zone (training with a new group of people).

Regular mental conditioning can help you achieve the mental agility needed to stay focused under duress. Including these near the end of training sessions or near the end of your working day is the best time to implement them as you are likely to be fatigued - I have always found training through fatigue to be the best way to condition my mind.

Creating a Distraction-Free Environment

During training sessions, minimizing external distractions can significantly improve focus. You need to provide a calm, distraction-free environment that promotes focus. Setting boundaries, practicing in more peaceful settings, or using noise-canceling headphones are some ways to prevent distractions during practice. The biggest distraction you can remove from your training sessions is your phone, although you may 'need' it for music or use it to aid your training, I am sure there are alternatives you can use. You don't realize how much time you waste when 'training' by checking your phone between rounds, try to leave your phone in another room and see how much more you can give to each session. Furthermore, try to limit phone use in everyday life.

Maintaining Great Physical Fitness

Physical fitness and mental attentiveness are directly correlated. The general function of the brain, including focus and attention, can be enhanced by regular aerobic exercise, weight training, and a nutritious diet. See below the benefits of maintaining great physical fitness:

- Regular aerobic exercise increases heart rate, which boosts blood flow and oxygen supply to the brain. Therefore, supporting brain cell function and the growth of new neurons.

- Regular exercise has been shown to improve memory and enhance learning abilities. The hippocampus, a region of the brain responsible for memory and learning, often grows as a result of regular aerobic activity.

- Regular physical activity increases the production of endorphins and serotonin, which are neurotransmitters that help improve mood, reduce stress, and alleviate anxiety.

- Studies suggest that regular training can help preserve cognitive function as we age. It may reduce age-related decline in memory, processing speed, and other cognitive domains.

Those benefits show that sticking to a consistent exercise routine significantly boosts many mental attributes. Getting started, just 2 boxing sessions a week can help you experience those benefits, to ensure that your exercise routine is most effective for maintaining great physical fitness, aim for at least 150 of moderate to intense exercise a week. Try to achieve a great balance of cardio, weight training, HIIT and mindful exercises like stretching or yoga. Exercise is only one half of maintaining great physical fitness, the fuel you give your body every single day is equally as important for these mental benefits.

- Nutrients like omega-3 fatty acids (found in fish, flaxseeds, and walnuts), antioxidants (in berries, vegetables, and green tea), and vitamins (like B vitamins and vitamin D) are crucial for maintaining brain structure and function.

- Protein-rich foods provide amino acids that help synthesize neurotransmitters like dopamine and serotonin, which regulate mood and cognitive function.

- Complex carbohydrates (whole grains, nuts, starchy veg) promote the release of serotonin, a neurotransmitter associated with feelings of well-being.

- Healthy fats (nuts, seeds, avocados, dark chocolate, eggs) support the production of essential brain chemicals. They provide steady energy and reduce brain fog, improving concentration, memory, and overall cognitive performance.

- Diets high in refined sugars and processed carbohydrates can lead to blood sugar spikes, which can impair cognitive function and increase the risk of developing neurodegenerative diseases.

Don't feel the need to attempt to make your diet perfect from the get-go as there is plenty to consider and it can become overwhelming. Start small by cutting out junk food, substituting simple carbs for complex carbs, increasing your lean protein intake and substituting unhealthy fats for healthy fats. Slowly build on your diet until you find what works for you.

I am sure you may already be aware of what you should eat and drink, and how often you should be exercising but you find it difficult to stick to it. It's much easier to have a takeaway instead of cooking, and it is much easier to miss a workout when you don't feel like doing it. Moments like these are when you build mental toughness, training your brain to say no to sweet treats is how you become disciplined enough to achieve your goals. So, make it easier for yourself. Stop filling your cupboards of unhealthy snacks, prepare healthy meals in advance so they are easier to cook when you are tired and plan your workouts in advance. When you get into a routine of eating well it becomes much easier to stick to it. When your diet is good, working out doesn't feel as much of a chore, you notice greater results in training.

Focused Drills and Sparring

When you integrate sparring sessions and tactics dedicated to concentration into your training you might enhance your focus during simulated fighting. Examples of this include precision target punching, memory drills like matching cards or attention switching like punching the bag and solving math equations. The brain can be trained to stay alert and active through exercises that require precise timing, quick reasoning, and concentrated attention spans. When you spar with a variety of partners and styles it prepares you for the unpredictability of actual fights.

Routine and Consistency

The key to growth with absolutely anything is consistency. All the greatest boxers in the world got to the top because they followed their training routine no matter what. You simply cannot expect to get good at anything if you only train when you feel like it, progress comes from doing the hard things when you don't feel like it. Many beginners fall into the trap of training as hard as they possibly can for the first few weeks and slowly drop the effort as they begin to feel fatigued or struggle to see any results.

My advice is to always start small and build up. Treat this as if you're running a marathon, you wouldn't run the first mile at a fast pace knowing you had 25 more miles to run. Even if you feel as if two boxing sessions a week isn't enough, focus on building the habit of regular exercise before ramping up the workload.

With that being said, aim for those small wins. Instead of trying to win a sparring session in your first week of boxing, simply aim to finish the 2 boxing sessions in that week. Aiming for a goal that is unrealistic straight off the bat will knock your confidence when you don't achieve it. Focus on being consistent as it allows for small, incremental progress.

These small wins build momentum over time, giving you the motivation and confidence to continue moving forward.

By maintaining consistency, you avoid the burnout that comes with sporadic bursts of effort. It helps regulate energy levels and makes progress feel manageable. This goes for adding random intense sessions to your workout routine, lets say you start with running 5k twice a week and you suddenly decide one day to run 15k to really push yourself, while you should push yourself with your training, such a jump in the intensity of training can be quite detrimental, it will take longer for you to recover from this sporadic session and could ruin the momentum you have already built. An alternative to implement progressive overload would be to start running 6k twice a week, or 5k 3 times a week.

Consistency leads to compounding effects over time. Much like interest on an investment, consistent effort creates exponential growth, where small improvements gradually build into significant accomplishments. Whether it's in sports, academics, or creative endeavors, the more consistent your practice, the more likely you are to achieve mastery. It is so simple, yet so many fail.

Keeping Composure Under Pressure

Being calm under duress is an important skill that you need to have as a boxer, and is also useful in many other areas of life. The fast-paced exchanges and high stakes in a boxing match necessitate a level of mental focus and control that allows you to think clearly and respond effectively. The ability to retain composure in the face of external pressures and internal stressors is referred to as resilience. Being cool might possibly mean the difference between sticking to a well-thought-out strategy and succumbing to the heat of the moment.

It is impossible to overstate how crucial poise is to boxing. If you are able to sustain composure under pressure you are better able to read your opponent's moves, anticipate blows, and launch counterattacks. Your capacity to think clearly allows you to stay on course, adapt to changing circumstances, and exploit your opponent's weaknesses. Conversely, a lack of poise can lead to rash decisions, ineffective attempts, and missed opportunities. An overly emotional or fearful combatant is more likely to make mistakes, be predictable, and put himself in danger.

Maintaining composure is critical during training and preparation, as well as during games. Your mental health may be harmed by the stress of hard training sessions, sparring matches, and the anticipation of future fights. By maintaining composure, you will be able to increasingly tolerate the rigors of training, stay focused on your goals, and consistently deliver exceptional performance. You can use a variety of tactics to become accustomed to pressure and develop your composure:

- **Exposure to high-pressure situations**: Experiencing high-pressure circumstances on a regular basis is one of the most efficient strategies to develop composure. This can be accomplished by engaging in hard sparring sessions, competitive drills, and participating in minor tournaments or displays. When you face pressure on a regular basis you become more familiar with it and learn to manage your reactions. This repetitive exposure gradually desensitizes you to the stress and anxiety associated with high-stakes situations.

- **Visualization and mental rehearsal**: Visualization is a powerful technique for building composure. By mentally rehearsing different scenarios and imagining yourself performing calmly and confidently under pressure, you can prepare your mind for actual high-pressure situations. Visualization helps create a mental blueprint for success, reducing anxiety and increasing self-assurance when facing real challenges.

- **Positive self-talk and affirmations**: The way you talk to yourself can influence your composure. Positive self-talk and affirmations can help counter negative thoughts and boost confidence. You can develop a repertoire of positive statements and repeat them during stressful moments to reinforce your belief in your abilities and maintain a calm mindset. For instance, phrases such as *'I am prepared'*, *'I can handle this'*, and *'I have outworked my competition'* can be powerful tools for remaining composed. Although, please note that for positive self talk to be effective you had to have put the appropriate effort in with training.

- **Developing a pre-fight routine**: When you have a regular pre-fight routine report you feel more in control and experience less nervousness. This regimen may consist of targeted warm-up activities, mental preparation methods, and relaxation as well as focus-enhancing rituals. In the face of pressure and uncertainty, a routine that is comfortable can provide senses of stability and predictability.

- **Embracing discomfort**: Being composed often involves learning to embrace discomfort rather than avoiding it. You should challenge yourself to step outside your comfort zone during training, pushing your physical and mental limits. By willingly facing discomfort and adversity, you can build resilience and confidence in your ability to handle pressure.

- **Reflecting on past experiences**: You can learn a great deal about maintaining composure by reflecting on past experiences. Analyzing previous fights and training sessions to identify moments of success and areas for improvement can provide valuable lessons. Understanding how you responded to pressure in the past and what strategies worked can help you develop more effective coping mechanisms for future challenges.

Finally, your capacity to remain cool under pressure has a significant impact on your performance, decision-making, and general success. You can develop the mental fortitude required to remain calm and focused in the ring by exposing yourself to high-pressure situations, practicing visualization and controlled breathing, engaging in positive self-talk, developing pre-fight routines, embracing discomfort, seeking support, and reflecting on past experiences.

Cognitive Training Exercises

Improving cognitive control through targeted workouts is an important part of your training regimen. Cognitive control refers to a variety of mental activities, including attention, working memory, and executive functions such as planning, decision-making, and problem-solving. Your focus, strategic thinking, and overall ring performance can be improved by increasing these cognitive talents. To obtain these benefits, you must integrate a number of exercises specifically designed to improve executive functioning and working memory into your practice.

Executive functions are high-level mental processes that help you plan, make decisions, manage your time, and complete complex activities. When you possess strong executive functions you have superior plan development, faster decision-making, and more efficient adaptation to the dynamic nature of a bout. Participating in games that demand planning and strategic thinking can assist you to improve on these important skills. Chess, for instance, is a great game for developing strategic thinking. It involves players' ability to plan several moves ahead, predict their opponent's actions, and adjust their approach accordingly. Similarly, other strategy-based games such as Checkers or Go can be useful.

Task switching, or the capacity to effectively transfer emphasis from one task to another, is critical in boxing, where you need to continually adjust to your opponent's moves and the shifting dynamics of the bout. Exercises requiring fast switching between things can help enhance this capacity. For example, you can train on various physical drills in quick succession, such as switching from a speed bag to shadowboxing to footwork drills, with the hope of transitioning your focus seamlessly and efficiently.

Inhibition control is the capacity to suppress spontaneous responses and retain discipline, which is critical for you to avoid overcommitting or falling into the opponent's traps. Tasks like the Stroop test, in which a person must identify the color of the word being displayed rather than the word itself (for example, the word "red" written in blue ink), might aid improve inhibitory control. Practicing this task improves your ability to concentrate on the important components of a match while ignoring distractions.

Effective time management is an important part of executive functioning. You can improve your time management skills by doing exercises that demand you to complete certain tasks within a set time constraint. Setting up a circuit training plan with each station taking no more than a minute will help you improve your efficiency and ability to manage time. Or simply plan out your day every morning and ensure you meet your own timings.

The cognitive apparatus in charge of momentarily storing and modifying information is known as working memory. You need a strong working memory to swiftly absorb information during a match, retain and execute intricate combinations, and stay aware of your opponent's patterns as well as your own. One popular exercise to improve working memory is the N-back task. In this task, you have to indicate when the current stimulus matches the one from N steps earlier in the sequence. The stimuli can be letters or numbers. To make this exercise more applicable to boxers' training, it can be modified to use various stimuli, including punch combos or footwork patterns.

Dual-task training helps improve working memory capacity by having participants do two tasks at once. For you, this can entail mixing a mental problem with a physical workout. For instance, you may perform fundamental math problems or practice combinations on the heavy bag while going over a series of numbers. When you receive this form of training you can become more useful at keeping and processing knowledge even when you are physically stressed.

A number of applications and memory-enhancing games are available. Games that need players to remember patterns, locations, or sequences might be helpful. A variety of exercises designed to improve various elements of cognitive function, including working memory, are available through apps like Lumosity and BrainHQ. You can play these games as part of your regular regimen to stay mentally sharp and agile.

An essential boxing talent is the ability to recognize and react to patterns, which requires working memory. Pattern recognition-based drills can be quite successful. A coach might design a set of punch combos or defensive techniques, for instance, and have you repeat them in the right sequence. Enhancing your working memory and capacity to remember while executing combinations during a match can be achieved by gradually lengthening and increasing the complexity of these patterns.

It demands persistence and ingenuity to integrate cognitive training exercises into your regular training regimen. It's vital to begin with easier chores and progressively increase the level of difficulty and intensity. The following advice can help you successfully include cognitive training in a boxing program:

- Start training sessions with mental primers and warm-ups that involve cognitive tasks. This could include basic dual-task exercises, strategic planning activities, or rapid memory games. Some examples of these tasks are below:

- 1) *Dribbling a ball while reciting words - Dribble a basketball while reciting words from a specific category (e.g., animals, fruits, cities). Try to increase the speed of dribbling or the difficulty of the category as you progress.*

- 2) *Flash memory - Flash a series of images, numbers, or words on a screen or cards for only a brief moment (e.g., 1-2 seconds). After the flash, try to recall the sequence or list of items shown. Increase the number of items as you get better.*

- Create boxing routines that combine mental and physical demands. For example, during footwork drills, your coach may call out combinations, and you must swiftly comprehend and carry out the instructions.

- 3) *Heavy bag with reaction cues - Hit the heavy bag using specific combinations while a coach calls out instructions like "duck," "slip," or "block" at random intervals. React to the verbal cues while maintaining your attack on the heavy bag.*

- Dedicate specific sessions each week to focus solely on cognitive training. This ensures that cognitive skills are given the same importance as physical conditioning and technical skills.

- Finally, you can include cognitive training exercises outside of boxing. Spend 10 minutes a day practicing puzzles, playing memory games or chess instead of gaming. This small habit can keep you in a steady routine of learning and developing your cognitive skills.

There's plenty to take in here, again start small with just one activity and work your way up, I recommend trying all the activities above at least once and continuously practice those which you feel are most beneficial.

Mindfulness Practice

Mindfulness, or the practice of remaining present and completely engaged at the moment, has received a lot of attention due to its capacity to improve cognitive control. This practice can help you focus more effectively, reduce stress, and increase general performance. When you integrate mindfulness practices into your routine you are able to improve your self-awareness, emotional management, and attentiveness, all of which are essential for success in the ring.

A mindfulness technique that can improve cognitive control is body scan meditation. Using this method, you mentally scan your entire body, focusing on any tense or uncomfortable spots. You might lay down or sit comfortably and slowly shift your focus to other body regions, starting with your feet and working your way up. You need to examine any sensations while concentrating on each location without passing judgment—just acknowledge them and move on. When you try this for the first time, you may feel like you need some strong drugs to make you feel anything, so I often instruct boxers to start with just the lower half of your body. Start at your feet, shift your mind to try and only feel for any tingling sensations, shaking or twitching. If you feel something, let the thought sit in your mind for a second and forget it before moving on to your calves. If you don't feel anything, keep trying parts of your body until you do notice a sensation.

The point of the body scan is to increase your awareness of your body. As you build a habit of finding physical sensations within your body, you connect more deeply with your body. Having this greater connection helps you respond to cues better, helps you relax on command and can even allow you to identify issues you have like poor posture, stiff joints and so on.

Mindful movement, like yoga or tai chi, mixes physical activity and meditation. These techniques involve a sequence of movements that emphasize breath and body awareness. Mindful movement can help you improve your balance, flexibility, and coordination, as well as enhance relaxation and mental clarity. Yoga, in particular, can benefit you by stretching and strengthening muscles, improving posture, as well as enhancing general physical and mental wellness.

Sitting meditation, also known as mindfulness meditation, takes place when you sit still and concentrate on your breath, a mantra, or a particular subject of focus. You can enhance your focus and emotional control by dedicating a daily period to practicing mindfulness meditation. Close your eyes, sit comfortably, and direct your mind to the focus you have selected for your meditation. When ideas come to mind, you should accept them without passing judgment and then slowly return your attention to your mantra or breathing. Consistently use this technique to become more adept at maintaining your composure and attention both inside and outside of the ring. You can also practice mindfulness in the gym by giving complete attention to each punch, move, and drill, and by not dwelling on the past or future, but on the now.

Visualization exercises can also be used to practice mindfulness. You can enhance your performance and prepare for contests by using visualization, which is the process of mentally practicing particular scenarios or outcomes. You need to picture yourself, for instance, walking into the ring, carrying out your plan, and deftly countering your opponent's actions. You may increase your focus and composure during a match, decrease your nervousness, and develop confidence by constantly imagining certain situations.

It takes commitment and persistence for you to integrate mindfulness exercises into your regimen. Starting with brief sessions and progressively extending them as you become more accustomed to the exercise can be beneficial. You may start off daily with just five minutes of body scan meditation or mindful breathing and work your way up to lengthier sessions. It is also critical to approach mindfulness with an open mind and a nonjudgmental attitude, acknowledging that it is natural for the mind to wander and ideas and emotions to arise.

Beyond the ring, mindfulness has numerous advantages for you. In addition to improving relationships, employment, and general wellness, mindfulness can also improve other aspects of life by generating more emotional control, self-awareness, and attention. When you engage in mindfulness, for instance, you may discover that you are able to manage stress and setbacks better, connect with your coach and colleagues more successfully, and strike a healthier balance between training and rest.

I have witnessed many boxers come through to my gym living a very stressed lifestyle, not because they have a difficult life but because they make their life more difficult than it needs to be. For example, at the gym if they make a mistake they tend to show their frustration and throw their gloves on the floor. While I understand it's annoying to mess up, what does that retaliation do? Usually an angry outburst just requires them to expend more energy and makes them look childish. Instead, take a second pause to think about what you are doing. Will an outburst truly help you correct your mistake? Or would it be better to take a few deep breaths and try again? Humans make mistakes, it's completely normal, what actually determines how mentally strong you are is how you bounce back from mistakes.

Channeling Aggression

Boxing is a high-stakes sport where emotions are strong and aggression and stress are commonplace. Not only is it essential to learn how to control anger and stress in the ring, but it's also critical to keep your physical and emotional well-being outside of it. Uncontrolled aggression in boxing can result in poor technique, hasty decisions, and a higher chance of damage. Uncontrolled aggression in other areas of life can result in embarrassment, legal trouble or other issues - so it's best we avoid that. Being able to regulate and use these intense feelings in a positive way might mean the difference between success and failure in life and boxing.

Boxing aggression, when properly managed and channeled, can be a formidable asset. It can boost your motivation, improve your competitive edge, and give you the energy needed to get through difficult battles. However, when aggression spirals out of control, it can have negative consequences. Unchecked aggressiveness frequently results in impulsive behaviors, poor technique, and penalties or disqualifications. For example, a fighter who allows their anger to fill their mind may abandon their fighting strategy, leading them to start swinging aimlessly at their opponent instead of conserving energy and striking them on the counter. Furthermore, extreme aggression can raise the risk of injury, both to yourself and to opponents, with long-term ramifications for your career.

The first step toward controlling violence is self-awareness. You must detect the factors that cause increased aggression, such as taunts from an opponent, a perceived unfair judgment by a referee, or irritation over a mistake. Once these triggers are understood, you can develop tactics for managing your emotional reactions. Deep breathing is a useful strategy. When your wrath rises, taking slow, deep breaths might help calm the nervous system and lessen the strength of the feeling. Practice in training so it's a tool you can use whenever you feel close to head loss.

Visualization is another strategy for managing aggressiveness. You might use visualization to mentally practice how you will react to situations that usually make you angry. Train your mind to respond positively in real-life situations by imagining yourself remaining calm and composed in the face of provocation.

The Power of Visualization

As previously stated, visualization is a mental technique that entails producing vivid, detailed images in the mind's eye to imitate events and consequences. This technique is more than just a tool for athletes; it's an effective strategy for everyone trying to improve performance, skills, and achieve their objectives. Visualization can be especially beneficial for boxers, helping you to psychologically prepare for fights, fine-tune your methods, and get the confidence required to excel both inside and outside the ring. At its foundation, visualization is about using the brain's capacity to generate and rehearse scenarios. You can effectively "train" your mind by clearly envisioning yourself performing specific acts or accomplishing specific objectives, in just the same way as you exercise your body.

Neuroscientific research has demonstrated that the brain frequently cannot distinguish between a real experience and a vividly imagined one, which is why you may feel confused after a night of heavy dreaming. This means that the mental rehearsal involved in visualization can lead to improvements in actual performance.

As a boxer, visualizing can take many different forms. A typical technique is performance visualization, in which you imagine yourself going through every phase of a match. This includes imagining the walk to the ring, the sounds of the crowd, the feel of the gloves, and the appearance of your opponent. You might mentally practice your tactics, envisioning yourself throwing precise punches and skillfully countering your opponent's moves.

By doing this frequently, you create a mental blueprint for success, which can help reduce worry and boost confidence during the actual battle. Another critical part of visualization is outcome visualization. This entails visualizing the desired outcome, such as having your hand raised in victory, feeling the pleasure of winning, or even standing atop a podium. By consistently visualizing positive outcomes, you can reinforce your belief in your ability to achieve your goals.

You should use a few fundamental tactics to begin visualizing success. First and foremost, you need to create a peaceful, distraction-free setting in which to fully immerse yourself in the visualization process. This ensures that your whole focus is on the mental images you are producing, resulting in a more in-depth and successful visualization experience. Finding a quiet place rid of distractions is a great setting to begin with.

Next, you should apply all of your senses during visualization. Rather than only seeing the events in your mind, you should endeavor to feel, hear, and even smell your imagined surroundings. This multisensory method improves the realism and impact of the visualization. For instance, you may envision the sound of the bell striking, the sensation of sweat-soaked gloves, and the roar of the crowd. The more detailed and vibrant the visualization, the more effective it will be in preparing the brain and body for actual performance.

Consistency is another important issue. To be effective, visualization, like any other skill, must be practiced consistently. You should employ visualization in your daily practice, setting aside a specified period regularly to mentally rehearse your performance and results. This could be done in the morning, as part of a pre-training routine, or even before bedtime. The idea is to make it a regular component of your training schedule. In addition to picturing favorable performances and outcomes, you can use visualization to defeat possible obstacles and setbacks. You can mentally prepare for various scenarios by thinking about how you would react to them, such as being hit with a heavy punch or dealing with weariness.

It is also helpful for you to imagine yourself in a calm and relaxed state. Stress and worry can have a bad impact on performance, so you should train your mind to be calm under pressure by visualizing yourself as composed and in control on a regular basis.

Outside of the ring, visualization can be used in a variety of situations. The same concepts apply whether you're preparing for a job interview or delivering a presentation. People who clearly imagine success and mentally rehearse the actions required to accomplish it can strengthen their confidence, improve their talents, and increase their chances of success.

Practical Exercises

For aspiring boxers and people looking to cultivate a boxing mentality, incorporating specific practical exercises into your training routine is crucial for developing both physical skills and mental toughness.

Shadow boxing stands out as a fundamental exercise that benefits boxers and those aiming to adopt a boxing mindset. By simulating a fight with an imaginary opponent, you can focus on honing your technique, footwork, and movement. This exercise not only improves your physical conditioning but also sharpens your mental acuity, visualization skills, and ability to remain composed under pressure. Embracing shadow boxing helps you enhance your focus, concentration, and mental fortitude, essential qualities for success in the ring and beyond. Below are some tips to aid your shadowboxing performance:

- *Visualize an opponent throwing punches at you.*
- *Mix up punches, combos and defensive techniques.*
- *Record yourself or train in a mirror.*
- *Set a timer and train with purpose.*

Engaging in heavy bag training is another valuable exercise for building strength, endurance, and confidence, while also refining your mental resilience and determination. Striking the heavy bag with intent and intensity allows you to practice punches, combinations, and defensive maneuvers effectively. The rhythmic sound of your punches landing on the bag can help you cultivate a disciplined and focused mindset, empowering you to overcome challenges both in boxing and in life.

Integrating interval training, like high-intensity interval training (HIIT), into your regimen is beneficial for improving cardiovascular fitness, stamina, and mental toughness. By pushing yourself during short bursts of intense exercise followed by brief rest periods, you can develop a strong work ethic, mental resilience, and the capacity to persevere through fatigue and adversity.

By consistently practicing shadow boxing, heavy bag training, and interval training, you can enhance your focus, discipline, resilience, and determination. These practical exercises not only elevate your boxing skills but also instill the mental attributes needed for success in the sport and in life. Embrace these exercises wholeheartedly to embody the grit, perseverance, and unwavering pursuit of excellence that define a true boxing mentality.

Remember that cognitive control is more than just managing your head during matches; it is about developing a disciplined, concentrated attitude to all parts of training and life. As you practice these abilities, you will notice major increases in your performance, resilience, and general wellness. Accept these methods, execute them consistently, and watch as they improve not only your boxing career but also your life. This chapter has created the framework for improving your mental game, providing you with the tools you need to face any opponent, whether in the ring or in daily life.

5. Increasing Your Value

You looked at methods to improve cognitive control in the last chapter, including mental preparation, mindfulness exercises, visualization techniques, and keeping cool under pressure. Expanding upon that basis, the present chapter centers on augmenting your worth to elevate your self-esteem and improve your boxing abilities. Here, you'll look at how confidence affects performance, offer self-esteem-boosting advice, and investigate the impact of self-worth. You'll also talk about how crucial it is to keep a growth mentality and work tirelessly. Let's take a look at the story of Tony.

Tony was a gifted boxer but suffered from low self-esteem brought on by self-doubt and criticism as a child. His performance and confidence in his abilities were hampered by comparing himself to others and dealing with internal negativity. Every time he made a mistake he told himself he was useless, before every competition he would tell everybody that he had no chance of winning and this self-doubt really limited his physical capabilities in the ring. While he was technically better than most of the boxers around him, other boxers had a competitive advantage over him as they fully believed in themselves more than Tony believed in himself.

Eventually, Tony became aware of how his negative mindset was damaging to his boxing ability, he realized that he needed to change if he wanted to have any success in the sport, so he took his focus away from physical training and prioritized his self esteem. He started by letting others know about his negative thinking patterns and how he doubted himself more often than not, following this he began asking for support, while he didn't like having to swallow his pride, those around him made an attempt to make Tony feel better about himself.

Tony was reminded of his great ability, the obstacles he managed to overcome in his life, he was invited out to activities and he built stronger relationships along the way. He started to feel good about himself, he felt as if what others were telling him were true and his negative thinking patterns became less common.

Next was the challenge to maintain his self esteem alone. He began journaling and creating attainable goals. As he built up a tally of these small wins, his self esteem started to match his talented boxing ability, Tony reached his greatest potential in the ring many months later with his newly discovered self-assurance and tenacity, winning matches and gaining respect. His narrative demonstrates how self-esteem problems may be resolved and small changes can result in amazing personal development and achievement. Anyone can increase their sense of worth by working consistently with dedication.

Affirmations are a good place to start when trying to overcome negative thinking. Affirmations are helpful, but true transformation necessitates working hard to strengthen your weak areas. Experience is essential; working out regularly and pushing yourself to the limit improves confidence and abilities. Although self-care and mindfulness are helpful, they should be used in addition to intense training.

Taking up hobbies, working on your physical appearance, and boxing on a regular basis can all help you feel more confident. It's important to accept flaws and avoid comparing yourself to other people. Establish limits to prevent going overboard and properly recognize accomplishments. Being confident comes from knowing your own abilities and being at ease with your identity, which is essential for winning fights.

Sustain your dissatisfaction to motivate ongoing development. Never stop trying to get better, no matter how good you are. It's crucial to outwork opponents; in boxing, the person who is willing to work the hardest usually wins. You may increase both your boxing performance and your sense of value by putting an emphasis on constant progress, accepting hard effort, and developing confidence via regular activity.

Understanding Self-Value

Value is essentially about one's sense of self-worth and self-esteem in connection to one's self-perception. It's your inner sense of value and merit, and it has a big influence on how you interact with the outside world and work for your objectives. The sense of your own worth is important in life and in boxing since it affects resilience, drive, and confidence. Anyone who wants to increase their performance and sense of contentment in life must realize that value is not fixed and can be enhanced with effort and commitment.

Value can be conceptualized as an internal measure of your own worth, potential, and abilities. It is influenced by a number of things, such as your own accomplishments, other people's opinions of yourself, and self-perception. Possessing a strong sense of worth is feeling confident in your abilities and knowing you deserve success and happiness. Conversely, low self-worth can lead to self-doubt, decreased motivation, and a reluctance to pursue goals, as seen in Tony's short story above.

The good news is that self-esteem is not an innate characteristic that you are born with or without. It is a dynamic trait that may be developed and improved with intentional effort and practice. Anyone can boost their self-esteem by honing their talents, challenging negative beliefs, and constantly pushing themselves to achieve more. Identifying and challenging negative ideas is one of the first stages of improving self-esteem.

These beliefs are frequently the result of previous experiences, cultural expectations, or internalized critiques. For example, you may assume that you are unworthy due to previous failures or negative comments from others. Recognizing negative tendencies and actively confronting them with positive affirmations might help you change your mentality. Affirmations, while useful, are not a substitute for action. Real improvement comes from actively working on your weaknesses and building on your strengths.

Experience is the foundation for developing self-worth. The more challenging and growth-oriented activities you participate in, the more confident you will become in your talents. You need to spend time in the gym practicing tactics and sparring with others. Each session expands your skill set, and as you advance, your confidence grows. This hands-on approach to learning and improvement outperforms simply thinking or talking about getting better.

Accepting faults is also essential. Nobody is flawless, and everyone has areas for improvement. Accepting your shortcomings as part of your unique individuality helps you to prioritize growth above perfection. This mindset adjustment alleviates the expectation to be faultless and instead promotes constant progress. No champion has ever got to where they are with lazy excuses or blaming others for their mistakes. When you make a mistake, own up to it and aim to fix it.

Setting boundaries is another important method. Learning to say no to things that do not line with your goals or values allows you to save energy and focus on what is truly important. This could include declining social gatherings in order to keep your training schedule or limiting how much others can influence your decisions.

Celebrating accomplishments appropriately is critical for sustaining your sense of worth. Rewarding yourself for hard work and accomplishments boosts motivation and recognizes your efforts. However, make sure that your rewards are in line with your aims. For example, instead of engaging in behaviors that may jeopardize your progress, reward yourself with a healthy treat or a calming activity after a challenging workout.

Maintaining a healthy level of dissatisfaction encourages continuous progress. Always striving for improvement, regardless of your existing position, ensures that you never become complacent. This mindset motivates you to push yourself and attain more success.

Success in boxing, as in life, frequently depends on who is ready to put up the most effort. While inherent skill is important, true champions are distinguished by their dedication and hard effort. Sacrificing time, enduring difficult training sessions, and remaining focused on your goals will eventually boost your self-esteem and lead to achievement.

Tips to Boost Self-Esteem

Building self-esteem is an important part of enhancing both your personal life and your boxing performance. Here are some practical ways to enhance your self-esteem:

- **Being kind to oneself is essential.** Everyone makes mistakes and has setbacks; what matters is how you address them. Instead of harsh self-criticism, practice self-compassion. Treat yourself with the same compassion and forgiveness that you would show a friend. Recognize your mistakes, learn from them, and move on.

- **Acknowledge your errors and draw lessons from them.** One of the biggest obstacles to self-esteem can be negative self-talk. Challenge any negative thoughts you may be having, such as *I can't do this* or *I'm not good enough*. Seek proof supporting these ideas, then use affirmations that are uplifting to refute them. For instance, swap out *'I'm terrible at this'* with *'I'm getting better every day'*.

- **Exercise regularly**. Regular physical activity, especially a discipline like boxing, helps you feel stronger and more capable. The physical changes in your body can lead to increased confidence in your appearance and abilities. Furthermore, you should look forward to your next workout, you should want to complete a difficult workout as you know just how good you are going to feel once you've completed it.

- **Reflect on your blessings**. By using this strategy, you may be able to shift your focus from what you lack to what you have, leading to a more optimistic outlook. Acknowledging your successes and the good aspects of your life can improve your overall well-being and self-worth. Write down the things you are grateful for and the progress you have made, remember many years ago you probably had nothing going for yourself so to have made it to where you are today is a great achievement.

- **Look as good as you can**. While it is important not to base your self-worth only on your appearance, grooming, dressing nicely, and keeping good hygiene can help you feel better about yourself and how others view you. If you can look into a mirror and a handsome, shredded man is looking right back at you then it makes you feel as if you are 'the man'. If you don't feel as if this is you, then you have something to work towards.

Getting the Balance Right

Experience is crucial for improving in any effort, including boxing. While techniques such as mindfulness and self-affirmation have their uses, they pale in comparison to the advantages of hands-on experience and effort. You must understand that excessive meditation or positive self-talk will not guarantee success in the ring. While these habits can help with mental health and recuperation, they should not replace the drive and determination required for tough training. Always prioritize putting in the time at the gym, pushing yourself to the limit, and honing your talents via hands-on experience.

Self-care is another critical component of maintaining optimum performance in boxing. Regular training sessions can be physically demanding, therefore, you must consider relaxation, recovery, and overall well-being. Hobbies and interests outside of boxing can help improve mental health and morale. Whether it's playing a musical instrument, painting, or spending time outside, having a variety of activities can provide balance and perspective, lowering the risk of burnout and increasing overall life happiness.

Boxing is not a quest for perfectionism, instead a quest for constant improvement. Therefore, don't let small errors in your sessions make it seem like you performed poorly. If you're too focused on making every movement flawless, you hesitate, overthink, and lose flow. Turn up to each session with the intention of performing better than your last session. As somebody who was a perfectionist in my younger years, I have spent so much time beating myself up for little mistakes and procrastinated in many areas of my life. Previously having this mindset is something I deeply regret.

Also, try by all means necessary to avoid making comparisons. Each person's boxing journey, skills, and weaknesses are unique. Comparing yourself to others can cause feelings of inadequacy and damage self-esteem. Instead, you should concentrate on your own growth and development, setting personal goals and standards for success.

Lastly, another essential component of personal well-being and self-care is setting boundaries. It is important for you to put your own needs first and not feel pressured to accept every opportunity or request that presents itself. To keep your balance and prevent burnout, you must learn to prioritize your own well-being and communicate your limits in an authoritative manner. Say no to things that drain you without adding value. Limit time with negative or toxic people. Set clear work-life separation (no emails after 8pm, no excessive overtime and so on). Don't feel guilty for putting yourself first, you are always more important than others.

Showing Your Confidence

A key component of boxing success is confidence. It's about having confidence in yourself and your talents, both inside and beyond the ring, rather than just physical skill. Even the most talented boxers can stumble when they lack confidence, doubting their choices and hesitating at key times. In contrast, a self-assured fighter exudes confidence, intimidating opponents and commanding admiration from onlookers.

Accepting yourself and your fighting style is the first step towards developing confidence in boxing. With unique qualities, shortcomings, and eccentricities, each boxer is unique. You should embrace your originality and make the most of what causes them to be different rather than attempting to imitate others. Embracing your own strengths can help you use a strong punch, quick reflexes, or an unconventional fighting position that translates to success in the ring. In fact, right now I want you to write down a list of your strengths both inside and outside the ring, dwell on these strengths and how they can benefit you in multiple ways. For example, having the ability to never give up can lead to a lifetime of consistent improvement, which is key for boxing.

Confidence also comes from knowing yourself and being comfortable in your own skin. You should take the time to understand your weaknesses also, both physically and mentally, and work on developing a positive self-image. This means accepting imperfections and embracing the raw, unfiltered version of yourself. People are drawn to authenticity, and when you embrace your real self, you will naturally display confidence and command attention.

Another important component of developing confidence and succeeding in boxing is outlasting the opposition. To become the best in a sport, you must possess talent alone; hard work, devotion, and relentless drive are required. You need to be prepared to give up things, such as social events or parties in order to focus on your goals. To be considered great both in boxing and life, you must be willing to do things your competition won't, whether that's training early hours of the morning, never taking a day off, spending time each day researching the sport, or making yourself known to the public.

You might obtain a competitive advantage and boost your self-confidence by outworking your opponents and putting in the work required to accomplish it. There are countless instances of boxers who have achieved greatness by working extremely hard and with unwavering desire. From Floyd Mayweather Jr.'s rigorous training schedule to Muhammad Ali's illustrious work ethic, these superstars inspire young boxers everywhere. Their stories remind you that success in boxing is not just about talent; it's about the willingness to work harder than anyone else and the unshakeable confidence that comes from knowing you've given your all in pursuit of your dreams.

To end this chapter, I have included many questions for you to consider. While you may not have an accurate answer as of right now, give your best effort to write something down in response to each question. Then, you can revisit these questions further down the line to see how you've developed as a boxer and person.

1. *Am I training with intention, or just going through the motions?*

2. *Do I embrace discomfort, or do I avoid difficult drills/rounds?*

3. *How do I respond to failure—do I learn from it or dwell on it?*

4. *If I had to fight myself, what weaknesses would I exploit?*

5. How do I handle fatigue—do I push through smartly or let it break me?

6. Am I surrounding myself with people who push me to be better?

7. How do I handle pressure—do I stay calm or let it overwhelm me?

8. What legacy or impact do I want to leave behind through my training and personal growth?

6. Mental Conditioning and Preparation

Failing to prepare is preparing to fail. I have been told that quote many times in my life and I have to admit it is probably the most accurate quote I have ever heard. Most of the time, boxing matches are won before they begin, it is the case of whoever trains the hardest wins, although there is room for bad luck and unexpected upsets, you should always do everything in your power to outwork your opposition.

The key to performance is mental conditioning. Mental toughness can be enhanced by desensitization through psychological warfare techniques and fear-setting activities. Growth requires reflection on feelings, instruction, victories, and defeats. You'll talk about overcoming setbacks with perseverance and constantly aiming for development without becoming perfectionists.

Your surroundings are crucial; you need the encouragement of friends and family as well as a comfortable place to practice and relax. The physical condition will be optimized with the use of performance enhancers including nutrition, hydration, and legal stimulants. Lastly, in order to help you find your identity and make sure your life is headed in the proper direction, you will pose personal questions.

Importance of Mental Conditioning and Preparation

In the tough and unforgiving world of boxing, where physical prowess and technique are paramount, mental training and preparation are critical. While power, speed, and ability are obviously important factors in a boxer's success, mental fortitude, focus, and resilience frequently distinguish the good from the great. In this section, you'll look at the importance of mental conditioning and preparation in boxing, and how your thinking can make all the difference in the ring. Mental conditioning refers to the process of training the mind to enhance mental toughness, focus, resilience, and emotional control in order to perform at a high level, especially under pressure. It involves mental preparation techniques that help individuals manage stress, stay motivated, and overcome obstacles or setbacks.

Pre-Fight Routine

As a boxer, managing performance anxiety is a typical problem. You can control this anxiousness and make sure you enter the ring with a composed, focused attitude by creating a pre-fight ritual. A boxer's well-structured regimen may differ greatly from another's, so it's critical to determine what suits you the best.

Before a fight, a lot of successful boxers adhere to certain traditions. These could be a predetermined warm-up routine, visualization exercises, or listening to music that either relaxes or energizes them. An example of visualization is practicing the fight in your head, seeing yourself using tactics, and coming out on top. This tactic, which gives the combat a familiar feel, can increase self-assurance and decrease nervousness.

As you learned before, controlled breathing exercises are another useful tactic. Taking slow, deep breaths can help lower anxiety and relax the nervous system. Focus and poise can also be improved by integrating mindfulness exercises like meditation. By engaging in these techniques, you can avoid becoming consumed by the stress of the situation and remain in the now.

Developing a customized pre-fight routine and trying out various tactics are essential. Find the ritual combination that best prepares you both physically and mentally, as what works for one fighter may not work for another. To reduce fear and improve your performance in the ring, keep in mind that the objective is to establish a sense of control and familiarity.

Example: Before a boxing match, the fighter mentally prepares in their locker room, visualizing success and calming nerves, possibly completing a quick breathing exercise also. They shadowbox to warm up, focusing on technique and strategy. They check over their gear to ensure they are ready to go. The coach offers final words of encouragement, and the fighter emerges, ready to face their opponent with determination and confidence.

Recovery

For any athlete, recovery is essential, but it's more critical in a physically demanding sport like boxing. In the sport, advanced recuperation methods can greatly improve longevity and performance. Maintaining optimal physical and mental health requires striking a balance between exerting yourself and taking time off. Overtraining can cause burnout, injuries, and a decline in performance, but the body can repair and strengthen itself with enough rest and recovery.

We have already discussed the importance of diet and hydration for the means of recovery between training sessions, but as you will be training hard during boxing sessions ensure to drink plenty of water each day (3 liters minimum) and replenish electrolytes after sweating them out, look for drinks high in sodium, potassium, magnesium, calcium and chloride. Sleep has also been discussed, you know you should aim to get 7-9 hours of sleep a night but if that is a struggle for you try the following:

- *Have a consistent sleep schedule, this helps your body fall asleep faster and enjoy deeper, more restful sleep.*
- *Keep your room cool at night.*
- *Have blackout curtains or wear an eye mask.*
- *Avoid caffeine 6+ hours before bed.*
- *Have a comfortable mattress and pillow, you spend roughly a third of your life sleeping so invest accordingly.*
- *Avoid heavy meals or intense exercise for a couple hours before bed, especially meals high in sugar.*

- *Avoid blue light an hour before bed, your bed should only be for sleeping and sex if you're that lucky.*
- *Try stretching, meditation or reading before bed.*
- *Monitor your sleep, smart watches help track sleep.*
- *Take magnesium supplements before sleeping.*

Active rehabilitation practices such as light jogging, yoga, or stretching can help enhance blood flow to muscles and speed up recovery. Ice baths, compression therapy, and massage can all help to alleviate muscle discomfort and inflammation. Listen to your body and alter your training intensity according to how you feel. Recovery is not a sign of weakness, but rather a deliberate component of an effective training plan.

Recovery from exercise is essential; foam rolling reduces muscular tension and frequent stretching preserves suppleness. Keeping an eye on your nutrition promotes healing, with a focus on consuming lots of protein to rebuild muscle. You can also think about recovery when training, wearing compression gear improves circulation and reduces muscle fatigue.

Turning Losses into Wins

Losses in boxing are unavoidable, just as they are in life. How you handle these failures impacts your long-term success. When you experience a loss, you must see it as an opportunity to learn and grow rather than a failure. Consider what went wrong and find areas for improvement. The following questions must run through your mind:

- *Did you become fatigued too quickly?*
- *Were there any technical mistakes?*
- *How was your mental state before and during the session/fight?*

Use these findings to tailor your training and strategies. It's common to feel frustrated, disappointed, or doubtful following a loss. Recognize these emotions, but don't let them overwhelm you. Remember that every champion has suffered defeats. The idea is to persevere and utilize each loss as a steppingstone toward future victories.

Constantly Strive for More

While it is critical to avoid the trap of perfectionism, aiming to go beyond your comfort zone is essential for ongoing progress with boxing. Set realistic, gradual goals that will push you. Whether it's raising your training intensity, learning a new technique, or improving your mental resilience, remain adaptable by constantly looking for methods to improve your skills and performance.

With the above being said, never downplay the basics, perfect your jab, footwork, and defense before moving to advanced techniques. After mastering the fundamentals, you can separate all aspects of boxing into areas which you can improve using training methods such as sparring with new opponents, cross-training, reflex training, flexibility training, using new boxing equipment, training in different settings, resistance band training and the list goes on. Having a list of all the attributes that make a great fighter with the training methods that improve each attribute will help you get well on your way to an advanced boxing ability.

You can also constantly strive for more in all areas of your life using the above strategy. If you're looking for greater financial income you could again list the attributes of a wealthy man and work towards building those attributes up, or if looking for a better dating life list the attributes of a charismatic man and work towards them. You can achieve anything you put your mind to, as long as you continue to push yourself and you never give up there is no reason why you can't achieve it. Continue to be curious and hungry for progress.

Environment

Your boxing success is greatly influenced by your surroundings. Encouragement and motivation can be obtained from your boxing community, friends, and family. Be in the company of encouraging people who will motivate you to reach your goals and have faith in you. Not only that but you should aim to surround yourself with winners. If you decide to stick by people who are lazy and unfit, you will have greater difficulty sticking to productive and healthy habits as their behaviors will easily rub off on you. While you can still hang around with these people, you may have to separate yourself from them regularly to truly commit to your goals. Please understand that going on this journey alone is much more challenging than you may think. As difficult as it may be to leave people behind to chase your goals, you are bound to meet winners as you go on this journey. Hanging around with winners won't automatically make you a winner but it makes training, nutritional eating and other difficult tasks or habits seem much more enjoyable. Finally, you can set up competitions with like-minded people to motivate each other further. All the greatest boxers have a strong team around them, so what's stopping you from creating new relationships with like-minded people at the gym and striving for greatness?

On the other hand, get rid of any distractions and bad influences that are impeding your development. Think about how well your training spaces are designed. You can concentrate entirely on your workouts in a well-equipped, quiet training room. In a similar vein, your home should be kept clean and tidy. If you have clothes scattered across the floor, unorganized cabinets and so forth it is likely to bring you extra stress, reduce your productivity and could be embarrassing for when you have guests. Your health and boxing performance should be influenced by every element of your surroundings. As you read about the boxing attitude, consider your surroundings.

1. Is everything orderly and conducive to concentration?

2. Is it set up for clarity and efficiency?

3. Do those in your immediate vicinity support your objectives?

Performance Enhancers

While you may be quick to consider steroids as the greatest performance enhancer, there are many alternatives that are legal and don't come with such consequences. I see many young men turn to illegal performance enhancers after struggling with making progress, when actually they haven't even bothered with the basics and haven't even given themselves enough time to see results.

Don't take shortcuts in life, just because you may be able to get in great shape much quicker on these drugs doesn't mean they actually do you any good. Taking illegal performance enhancers could lead to disqualification on drug tests, many health issues and reputational damage. So after you have made a consistent effort to your training routine and have maintained great nutrition, you can take into consideration the following legal performance enhancers.

Vitamins, electrolytes, and protein powders are examples of legal supplements that might help your training program. Taking electrolyte supplements are most useful first thing when you wake up and after a workout. Multivitamin tablets are fairly cheap and one a day is great help. Protein powders after a workout also are great for boosting recovery. Just 100mg of caffeine before a workout can improve performance and focus as well. As long as you don't take too much caffeine each day (avoid over 400mg a day) and get it from healthy sources (avoid sugary energy drinks) it will be a great enhancer. Before trying caffeine, be sure to carry out your own research and consult with a doctor if you have any worries.

Creatine is a great natural performance enhancer that boosts energy production in muscles, helping with strength, endurance, and recovery, it is also well researched and safe for consumption. Taking 3-5g a day benefits cognitive function, boosts ATP production and supports muscle growth. Just remember to keep on top of hydration as creatine increases water retention in your muscles.

Nicotine is proven to improve focus, memory, and reaction time by stimulating neurotransmitters like dopamine and acetylcholine. Nicotine is a stimulant, similar to caffeine, that increases brain activity, temporarily boosts your mood and reduces stress. However, the issue with nicotine is that it is mostly consumed by smoking or vaping which come with great health risks as the chemicals are damaging to your lungs and oral health. Great alternatives include nicotine pouches, nicotine gum or nicotine lozenges, as they are less harmful. Furthermore, nicotine is highly addictive and increases blood pressure, so proceed with caution. Do your own research and consult with a doctor before trying.

Psychological Warfare

Psychological warfare in boxing refers to the use of mental tactics and mind games to gain an advantage over an opponent, often before the fight even begins. The goal is to unsettle or distract the opponent, influencing their confidence, decision-making, and emotional state during the fight. It's a strategic tool that goes beyond physical conditioning, aiming to affect the mental state of the opponent. So, what tactics could you use?

The goal of trash talk is to provoke or intimidate the opponent by undermining their confidence, making them feel disrespected or pressured. This is done by insulting your opponent's skills, personal life, or previous performances. This can get into your opponent's head, making them lose focus, feel angered, or second-guess their ability. This tactic works depending on who you are as a person, if you prefer to be respectful then it's best to avoid this tactic, however, if you are willing to do anything in your power to win then give it a go. Remember, trash talk is just a part of boxing so if you are able to dish it out, ensure you can take it also. Although not a boxer, Conor McGregor is a perfect example of a successful trash talker.

Following trash talk we have mind games, the purpose is to create a mental advantage by controlling the narrative or gaining the upper hand before the physical confrontation. If the opponent begins to feel overwhelmed or underprepared mentally, it can disrupt their performance. Good examples include:

- *Staring down your opponent in the weigh-in to show dominance.*
- *Psyching them out by acting overly confident or nonchalant.*

- *Publicly questioning their heart or dedication to the sport.*

Another method is to display dominance or confidence, how you go about this is down to you. If you project overwhelming confidence, you make the opponent question their ability to compete. Great ways to do this include entering the ring with an intimidating posture, showing physical superiority, or being unfazed by an opponent's antics.

If you are a less outgoing person, acting calm under pressure could be a great tactic to confuse the opponent by not revealing emotions or maintaining composure during high-pressure situations. Keeping a stoic expression while getting hit or taunted, or not showing any signs of pain or fear.

Finally, the silent treatment could be a great way to get in your opponent's head. By not engaging in conversation or banter it can make your opponent feel like they are irrelevant or beneath you. Yet again, depending on the situation determines how well this pays off.

Yet again, psychological warfare is a case of trial and error, you may have to try multiple tactics until you discover what works for you, it may be best to approach each fight with a different tactic to remain unpredictable. It is worth noting that your opponents are going to do the exact same thing to you, so be prepared for it, don't take their bait and appear mentally stronger than they are.

Self-Reflective Questions

Self-reflection is an effective strategy for both career and personal development. You can gain a better understanding of your motives, anxieties, and places for progress by posing tough questions to yourself. Consider inquiries such as: What are the secrets you are keeping from both yourself and the world? Which feelings are you not expecting to experience? Are underlying doubts preventing you from achieving your boxing goals, or are you genuinely committed to them?

These inquiries promote more honesty and self-awareness. Gaining insight into your inner terrain will enable you to confront repressed anxieties and phobias and move toward more genuine and targeted advancement. You can keep in step with your objectives and make sure that your actions are guiding you in the right path by engaging in regular self-reflection. To improve their boxing mindset, fighters can ask themselves the following self-reflective questions:

1. When things get tough, do I stay calm and focused or do I let my feelings get the better of me?

2. Am I receptive to my teammates' and coaches' helpful criticism and comments?

3. How do I deal with uncertainty and dread before I get into the ring?

4. Do I know exactly what my boxing strengths and limitations are?

5. Have I trained and prepared in a disciplined and consistent manner?

6. Do I hold myself responsible for reaching the exact goals I set for myself in both training and competition?

7. How can I maintain my desire and motivation when things go tough in my boxing journey?

8. Can I withstand adversity and challenge opponents with mental toughness and resilience?

9. How do I go about taking chances and making choices in the ring?

10. Do I envision winning and happy endings before battles?

11. Do I play well in both wins and losses as a sportsman?

12. How can I develop self-assurance and faith in my boxing prowess?

13. Do I value my mind and body by prioritizing rest, recovery, and self-care?

14. How do I handle outside demands and distractions that could impair my performance?

15. Do I help and encourage people in my boxing community?

16. How can my fighting style strike a balance between control and aggression?

17. How do my boxing ideals and principles influence my mindset both inside and outside of the ring?

You can learn a great deal about your own mindset, actions, and attitudes toward the sport by thinking about these questions on a frequent basis and looking for honest responses. Increased performance, personal development, and an all-around stronger boxing mindset can result from this self-awareness.

You've covered the essential elements of mental training and boxing preparation in this chapter. Building on the knowledge from your earlier lesson, it is evident that mental toughness is just as important to success in the ring as physical prowess. By highlighting the significance of recuperation, you acknowledge that long-term health and optimal performance depend on striking a balance between exertion and rest.

You also discussed the importance of a pre-fight exercise regimen designed to address anxiety related to fighting performance. Given that every boxer is different, you obtained knowledge on the significance of developing a customized routine that maximizes confidence and attention.

You are further prepared to withstand the demands of the ring by participating in desensitization exercises, which push you to frequently step outside of your comfort zones. Resilience and flexibility are forged by this relentless pursuit of discomfort and are essential qualities for each great boxer.

As you proceed, keep in mind that mental training and readiness are ongoing endeavors. They demand commitment, self-control, and the courage to face and conquer obstacles. You'll be more prepared to handle the rigors of boxing and achieve not only success in the ring but also personal development and fulfillment if you include these ideas in your practice.

7. Beyond the Ring

The last chapter took you through the essentials of mental training and boxing readiness. You discovered that being successful in the ring takes more than brute force; it takes a comprehensive strategy that includes conditioning, mental toughness training, desensitization, and frequent introspection. You stressed the significance of creating customized routines to address performance anxiety, striking a balance between rigorous training and enough rest, and never stopping the pursuit of growth. The foundation of a great boxing career is made up of these components, which are resilience, mental toughness, and strategic thinking.

This chapter will look at how to attain personal greatness in all facets of life by using the mental and physical discipline developed in the boxing ring. The emphasis will be on using boxing concepts to achieve success in both your personal and professional life. You will learn the definition of personal excellence and how it might be evaluated in addition to sporting accomplishments. The chapter will also offer motivation and useful insights by looking at the success stories of people who have used a boxing mentality to overcome challenges and achieve new heights.

Translating Boxing Principles into Personal Success

Translating boxing principles into personal and professional success involves applying key strategies from the sport to achieve goals efficiently. Here are some key principles:

1. **Discipline**: Just as boxers adhere to strict training regimes, maintaining discipline in personal and professional life is crucial for success. This could be as simple as waking up at the same time every morning without snoozing, sticking to a work schedule like the Pomodoro Technique (work for 25-50 minutes, then take a 5-10 min break), committing to continuous learning, sticking to a financial budget and so on.

2. **Resilience**: In boxing, fighters must endure setbacks and keep fighting. Similarly, in personal and professional endeavors, resilience in the face of challenges is vital. Learning from failures and bouncing back stronger is key. Seeking rejection is a great way to build resilience outside of boxing, the idea is to intentionally put yourself in situations

where rejection is likely, so you become desensitized to failure and learn to handle setbacks with ease

3. **Strategy**: Boxing matches require strategic planning to outmaneuver opponents. In personal and professional life, having a clear plan and adapting it as needed can lead to success. Strategy mostly comes from studying, therefore look at historical trends in your personal life, observe the patterns of successful people and stay informed by reading books or following experts.

4. **Focus**: Boxers must stay focused during fights to react quickly and make split-second decisions. Applying this level of focus in personal and professional tasks can improve efficiency and productivity. Train your brain for deep work, block out 2-4 hours of deep focus time daily, start small and train your brain to focus for longer periods and most importantly avoid multitasking, you are much more productive focusing on one task at a time.

5. **Continuous improvement**: Boxers constantly train to enhance their skills. Similarly, seeking opportunities for growth and learning in personal and professional life is essential for long-term success. At

this stage of the guide, I am sure you are aware of the many ways you can commit to continuous improvement, so get started with it and enjoy the challenge.

Achieving Personal Excellence

Personal excellence is a concept that goes beyond simply being competent or successful in any given sector. It is about striving for constant growth, becoming the best version of yourself, and sustaining high standards in all parts of life. Personal excellence entails a dedication to development, the pursuit of high-quality outcomes, and the persistent application of your values and ideals. It entails establishing and maintaining high standards for yourself in a variety of areas, including physical health, mental well-being, emotional intelligence, and social relationships.

One of the most important parts of personal excellence is self-awareness. This entails acknowledging your own talents and flaws, identifying opportunities for progress, and being open about your abilities. It also entails being aware of your values and ensuring that your behaviors and decisions are consistent with those ideals. If your senses of purpose and direction are clear, you are better able to make educated decisions that contribute to your overall development.

Personal excellence requires effective time management and prioritizing. Efficient time management allows you to juggle your personal and professional duties while still making time for self-care and recreational pursuits.

Prioritizing tasks based on your importance and urgency allows you to focus on what is actually important while avoiding becoming overwhelmed by less relevant activities.

Personal excellence relies heavily on emotional intelligence. This entails being aware of and managing your own emotions, as well as comprehending and empathizing with the feelings of others. High emotional intelligence improves relationships, communication, and conflict resolution. It allows you to manage social situations with elegance and composure, creating a positive and supportive environment both personally and professionally.

Personal excellence relies on continuous learning and self-improvement. This entails remaining curious, acquiring new knowledge and abilities, and being open to new experiences. Lifelong learning not only improves your abilities but also keeps the mind alert and engaged. It entails taking classes, reading books, attending seminars, and participating in activities that create growth and development.

Ultimately, personal achievement is an adventure, not a destination. It is about aspiring to be the best version of yourself, setting lofty goals, and working tirelessly to achieve them. It takes a comprehensive approach to self-improvement that includes physical health, mental wellness, emotional intelligence, and social relationships.

To achieve personal excellence is tough, which is why so many people cannot do it. This is your call to show everybody that you are simply better than them. Don't be arrogant about it but reflect on all the obstacles you have overcome and remind yourself just how excellent you are. While comparison to others can be very motivating, think of this, no matter what position you are in, your life will be tough. Being unhealthy is tough as it comes with health issues and feelings of low self worth, being healthy is tough as you have to stick to healthy habits. Being poor is tough as it can be stressful to pay the bills, whereas being rich is tough as it can be stressful to stick to a routine of consistent work for many years. You get the idea, your life will be difficult no matter what, so would you rather be at a disadvantage in life struggling to get by or be at an advantage in life having struggled to get to that position?

Success Stories

Success stories about people who have developed mental toughness provide great motivation and useful lessons. These examples demonstrate how tenacity, determination, and a strong mentality can lead to extraordinary accomplishments, even in the face of enormous obstacles. Here are some noteworthy examples.

Michael Jordan: The Basketball Legend

Michael Jordan's rise to become one of the greatest basketball players of all time exemplifies the importance of mental toughness. Jordan suffered a significant setback early in his career when he was cut from his high school's varsity basketball squad. Jordan turned his disappointment into inspiration rather than a setback. He dedicated himself to consistent practice, perfecting his skills and improving his game. Jordan's tenure with the Chicago Bulls is notable for his outstanding work ethic, competitive spirit, and ability to execute under duress. He led the Bulls to six NBA titles and won five MVP honors. Jordan's famous phrase, "I've failed over and over in my life. And that is why I succeed," sums up his belief that failures are stepping stones to success. His story underscores the importance of resilience and the willingness to learn from setbacks.

Nelson Mandela: A Symbol of Resilience and Strength

Nelson Mandela's life exemplifies mental toughness in the face of great adversity. Mandela, an amateur boxer, served 27 years in prison for his anti-apartheid activities in South Africa. Despite the difficult conditions and extended separation from his family, Mandela remained committed to justice and equality.

Following his release, Mandela was instrumental in eliminating apartheid and promoting unity in South Africa. He became the nation's first black president and a global emblem of fortitude and moral strength. Mandela's capacity to endure prolonged suffering without losing hope or abandoning his convictions exemplifies the exceptional strength of mental toughness.

Bethany Hamilton: Overcoming Physical and Emotional Trauma

Bethany Hamilton's tale is one of incredible resilience and mental power. Hamilton, 13, was a promising young surfer until she lost her left arm in a shark attack. Many people assumed Hamilton's surfing career had ended, but she was determined to return to the sport she loved.

Within a month of the attack, Hamilton was back in the water, modifying her style to surf with one arm. She went on to win national surfing championships and became an inspiration to others through her autobiography, *Soul Surfer*, and its film adaptation. Hamilton's biography demonstrates how mental toughness may help people overcome physical and emotional trauma to reach success.

David Goggins: The Epitome of Mental Toughness

David Goggins, a former Navy SEAL and ultra-endurance athlete, is renowned for his exceptional mental fortitude. Poverty, abuse, and obesity dominated Goggins' early existence. However, he altered himself through sheer willpower and unwavering discipline. He reduced over 100 pounds in three months to qualify for Navy SEAL training, one of the most demanding military schools in the world.

Goggins went on to run other ultramarathons, triathlons, and other extreme endurance events. He holds the Guinness World Record for the most pull-ups done in 24 hours. Goggins' memoir, *Can't Hurt Me*, covers his path and emphasizes the "40% rule"—the idea that when you believe you're finished, you're only at 40% of your potential. His narrative is a strong testament to the limits of human endurance and the role of mental toughness in pushing beyond perceived boundaries.

Elon Musk: Perseverance in the Pursuit of Innovation

Elon Musk, the CEO of SpaceX and Tesla, is renowned for his unchanging perseverance and mental toughness when pursuing lofty objectives. Musk's endeavors have encountered many obstacles, such as multiple failed rocket launches and production setbacks, but he has persisted in his vision of advancing space exploration and sustainable energy.

Musk's story, which emphasizes the value of resilience, innovation, and unwavering belief in one's mission, has resulted in significant accomplishments like the successful launch of reusable rockets and the mass production of electric vehicles.

These success tales show that mental toughness is an essential component in achieving greatness. Whether conquering personal difficulties, enduring physical hurdles, or persevering through professional losses, these people demonstrate the power of perseverance, tenacity, and a strong attitude. Their adventures provide valuable insights and inspiration for anybody looking to develop mental toughness and achieve personal goals.

Boxing Mentality in Daily Life

The boxing mindset emphasizes strategy, resiliency, and discipline. This kind of thinking can be used in real life to take on obstacles head-on and persevere through difficult times. Like a fighter in the ring, you must be prepared to adjust to any circumstance and maintain focus and determination.

For instance, in your professional life, tackle challenges with the same tenacity as a boxer vying for a championship. Remain resolute in your work ethic, overcome obstacles, and always have a strategy in place to reach your objectives.

The boxing mindset in relationships refers to defending your own interests, being composed in the face of disagreement, and planning how to create lasting bonds with other people.

When it comes to personal development, adopt the mindset of a boxer getting ready for a major match. To become the best version of yourself, step outside of your comfort zone, maintain discipline in your routines, and plan ahead.

All things considered, having a boxing attitude in all facets of life entails being methodical, tough, and astute. If you approach problems with a fighter's mentality, you'll be more capable of overcoming setbacks and succeeding.

In addition, maintaining a humble foundation, asking mentors for advice, and realizing the value of building a solid support network are essential steps on the path to being a wonderful person off the mat. You can gain by surrounding yourself with positive influences that motivate and guide you to realize your full potential, just as boxers do from their trainers and teammates.

Finally, by internalizing the fundamental principles of boxing—resilience, discipline, and mental toughness—you open the door to realizing your full potential and attaining personal greatness. Your journey outside of the ring is evidence of the life-changing potential of adopting a boxing mentality, enabling you to face life's challenges with bravery, tenacity, and a powerful commitment to excellence.

Conclusion

As we wind down, *Boxing Mentality*, it's important to reflect on our shared journey and knowledge. This guide has been thoughtfully prepared to provide you with the tools and insights you need to change your habits, mentality, restructure your attitude, and achieve long-term personal and professional success.

We talked about how important it is to develop a strong mentality similar to that of boxing champions like Ali in Chapter 1. You can build the mental toughness necessary for success in any endeavor by practicing dedication, perseverance, and unwavering commitment.

Chapter 2's topic, which examined the idea of facing oneself as the harshest challenger, was *Your Toughest Opponent*. To achieve personal growth and overcome obstacles, you must face your fears, doubts, and self-limiting beliefs. This can be compared to the boxing ring where opponents test a fighter's skills and resolve. By adopting the resilience and determination of boxing legends, you can triumph over your inner struggles and emerge stronger, equipped to conquer challenges and reach your full potential.

Chapter 3 emphasized the need to seek results through consistent approaches. By moving our focus from outcomes to the everyday behaviors and routines that drive success, we learned how to foster a growth mindset and develop habits that correspond with our long-term objectives. This chapter demonstrated the transformative power of minor, incremental adjustments.

Building on this, Chapter 4 presented ways to improve cognitive control. We looked at ways to enhance concentration, control emotions, and stay calm under pressure. The chapter stressed the importance of mindfulness, cognitive training exercises, and visualization in bolstering our mental abilities.

In Chapter 5, we discussed the significance of developing our self-esteem and confidence. We talked about how to boost self-esteem using affirmations, challenge negative attitudes, and gain experience. The chapter also discussed the power of confidence and the need to push past our comfort zones.

Going on to Chapter 6, the topic of mental training and readiness was covered. Recovery, pre-fight routines, and coping mechanisms for worry and dread were all covered. We talked about the value of self-reflection, overcoming setbacks with perseverance, and aiming for constant progress.

We applied the life lessons we gained in the boxing ring to all facets of life in Chapter 7. We talked about using the boxing mentality—which is marked by perseverance, self-control, and concentration—to succeed both personally and professionally. We demonstrated the general relevance of these ideas with anecdotes of people who overcame adversity by using mental toughness.

As we approach the end of this guide, it is important to emphasize the main idea that has run throughout all of the chapters: The influence of our thoughts on our behaviors and, eventually, our fate. The techniques and insights offered in this book are useful tools that will empower you to take charge of your life and bring about long-lasting change, not just theories.

It is appropriate for us to review the main ideas of this book at this point by thinking back on the lessons we have learned. The only way to accomplish this is to examine the stories of some of the world's best boxers.

It is a known fact that there is a lot of information and inspiration in the boxing scene that may be applied outside of the ring. In addition to showcasing their physical skill, fighters like Floyd Mayweather, Mike Tyson, and Muhammad Ali have also shown incredible mental toughness and discipline, qualities that are admirable in many facets of life.

Floyd Mayweather, who is renowned for his unbeaten record and defensive prowess, is a prime example of the value of commitment and perseverance in reaching objectives. Mayweather is a living example of the value of perseverance due to his unwavering training schedule and dedication to honing his craft. By using his work ethic to improve mental conditioning or kick a particular habit, people can overcome obstacles by putting in constant effort and showing steadfast devotion.

Mike Tyson, a powerful and intimidating fighter in his heyday, has tasted both victories and defeats (and ears) throughout his career. His experience teaches a tremendous lesson about resilience and the ability to overcome hardship. Tyson's recovery from personal and professional setbacks exemplifies the value of patience and mental strength in overcoming challenges and attaining success.

Muhammad Ali, known for his charming demeanor and legendary boxing abilities, exemplified the strength of self-belief and mental tenacity. Ali's catchphrase, "I am the greatest," exemplifies his unshakeable confidence and positive attitude. Individuals can create a winning mindset by embracing Ali's self-assurance and conviction in themselves, propelling them with an unyielding drive toward their larger life goals.

Whether you want to break a specific habit, enhance your mental conditioning, or apply the boxing mentality to your overall life goals, the insights learned from these boxing superstars can be a valuable resource. Individuals can use Mayweather's determination, Tyson's resilience, and Ali's self-belief as inspiration to manage hurdles, overcome personal limitations, and achieve success in all parts of life. Remember that the path to breaking a habit and attaining long-term change is not linear. It demands dedication, self-reflection, and the resolve to see failures as chances for growth. The techniques and principles presented in this guide are meant to be integrated into your daily life, acting as a compass to navigate the complexities of habit transformation.

As you move forward, remember the value of consistency, resilience, and a growth attitude. Celebrate your success, no matter how modest, and persevere in your pursuit of personal perfection. Whether you want to break a specific habit, better your mental conditioning, or apply the boxing mentality to your overall life goals, the insights obtained from this guide will be a valuable resource.

Thank you for starting this adventure and may the knowledge and tactics you've gained inspire you to live the life you want, full of resilience, purpose, and unflinching drive. The path ahead is yours to conquer; approach it with the confidence and mental toughness of a boxing champion.

Remember, the process of change is not always linear, and it is okay to stumble along the way. What matters most is your willingness to get back up, learn from your experiences, and keep moving forward. Embrace each step of your journey with patience, curiosity, and unwavering belief in your ability to create the life you desire.

Thank you for allowing *Boxing Mentality* to be a part of your journey. May the lessons and insights gained from this guide empower you to break free from old habits, cultivate new ones, and live a life that reflects your true potential. Your journey toward lasting change begins now—take it one step at a time, and let each moment be a testament to your strength and resilience.

References

Ahrens, J. (2023, June 6). *Overcoming imposter syndrome*. Institute of Public Administration Australia (IPAA). https://www.ipaa.org.au/overcoming-imposter-syndrome/

Blystone, D. (2024, February 15). *How elon musk became elon musk*. Investopedia. https://www.investopedia.com/articles/personal-finance/061015/how-elon-musk-became-elon-musk.asp

Collins, N. (2019). Floyd mayweather, jr. | biography & facts. In *Encyclopædia Britannica*. https://www.britannica.com/biography/Floyd-Mayweather-Jr

Collins, N. (2020). Manny pacquiao | biography, facts, & notable fights | britannica. In *Encyclopædia Britannica*. https://www.britannica.com/biography/Manny-Pacquiao

Contenders Boxing Studio. (2023). *Building confidence and discipline through boxing training*. Contenders

Boxing Studio. https://contenders.ca/building-confidence-and-discipline-through-boxing-training/

Haigh, M. (2024). *The foundations of mental toughness.* ATHLETE TOUGH. https://athletetough.com/the-foundations-of-mental-toughness/. 4.

Hamilton, B. (2019). *Bethany's story | bethany hamilton.* Bethany Hamilton; Soul Surfer & Co. https://bethanyhamilton.com/biography/

Hauser, T. (2018). Muhammad ali. In *Encyclopædia Britannica.* Britannica. https://www.britannica.com/biography/Muhammad-Ali-boxer

Qoutefancy. (2024). *Top 25 alex hormozi quotes (2024 update) - quotefancy.* Quotefancy.com. https://quotefancy.com/alex-hormozi-quotes

The Editors of Encyclopedia Britannica. (2019). Mike tyson | biography, record, & facts. In *Encyclopædia Britannica.* https://www.britannica.com/biography/Mike-Tyson

Walla, P. (2023, June 8). *Learnings from life of david goggins, the strongest man alive.* Medium.

https://bootcamp.uxdesign.cc/from-ordinary-to-extraordinary-the-inspiring-tale-of-david-goggins-1027e572742e

WBA Press. (2019, July 18). *Mandela and his relationship with boxing.* World Boxing Association. https://www.wbaboxing.com/boxing-news/mandela-and-his-relationship-with-boxing

www.ingramcontent.com/pod-product-compliance
Lightning Source LLC
Chambersburg PA
CBHW030449100526
44580CB00002B/54